How to Make & Keep Friends:

Tips for Teens on Life and Social Success

Donna Shea and Nadine Briggs

How to Make & Keep Friends: Tips for Teens on Life and
Social Success

Copyright © 2017 by Donna Shea and Nadine Briggs

ISBN-13: 978-0997280838

ISBN-10: 0997280838

It is with our immense pleasure and gratitude that we dedicate this work to the members of the Maynard, Massachusetts Class of 2017 who candidly and openly shared their social experiences with us and were instrumental in making this book a reality.

We also wish to acknowledge all the people who helped us make this book the best it can be. We want to thank our illustrator, Ryan Flynn, for his work on the cover design and our editor, Rachel Cohen, for always making us grammatically look our best!

We especially want to thank all our Red Pen Readers, those adults and teens who read our draft and gave us terrific feedback for this published version. A big thank you goes out from us to:

Alex	Matthew
Aniket	Michael
Carol	Michele
Coryn	Nick
Fiona	Norah
James	Owen
Jeanne	Pierce
Jesse	Shane
Lori	Sheila
Madelyn	Sofia

Contents

Introduction   1

Section 1: Self

1. Personal Hygiene   4

2. Sleeping and Eating Habits   6

3. Personal Power   9

4. Optimism   13

5. Standing Your Ground   17

6. Building Self-Confidence   20

7. Defend and Deflect   23

8. Mistakes and Apologies   26

9. Filtering Your Words   30

10. Uniqueness   33

11. Fitting In   35

12. Managing Strong Feelings   38

13. A Lack of Motivation   42

Section 2: Others

14. The Ice Cream Social   46

15. Real Friends Checklist   50

16. Changing Friendships and Flip Flop   52
    Friends

17. Finding Friends   55

18. Adjusting to Social Feedback   58

19. When Others Annoy You   62

20. Crushes and Flirting   65

21. Dating and Sexuality   69

22. Being Excluded, Ignored, or Rejected   72

23. Considering Another Point of View   75

24. Conversation Skills   78

25. Social Drama   81

26. Bullying and Meanness   84

27. Conflicts and Disagreements   87

28. Teens' Rights versus Parents' Rights   90

29. Siblings   93

30. Authority Figures   96

31. Peer Pressure   99

32. Attending Funerals and Mourning   103

Section 3: Online and Social Media

33. The Almighty Internet   107

34. Privacy and Personal Information   110

35. Friending and Netiquette   114

36. Online Presence   117

37. Gaming   120

38. Sharing Too Much and Annoying Others   123

39. Offline Meeting and Online Predators   126

40. Cyberbullying   128

Section 4: The Bigger World of College, Work, and Adulthood

41. Introductions   131

42. Interviews   134

43. Babysitting   137

44. Appointments   140

45. Driving   142

46. Doorways, Hallways, and Elevators   145

47. Accepting Criticism   147

48. Telephone Etiquette   149

49. Professional Conduct and Work Ethic   151

50. Fear of Adulthood   155

Afterword   158

Introduction

We are happy that you found our book. Being a teenager isn't always easy, and navigating friendships and relationships can be especially difficult for teens.

Our goal in writing this book was to help make the social journey through the teenage years an easier one for you. This time in your life can feel both exciting and difficult. There are some challenges that every teen experiences. These include:

- **Changing Brains**
- **Changing Bodies**
- **Strong Emotions**
- **Understanding Yourself**
- **Developing a Value System**
- **Awkwardness**
- **Changing Friendships**
- **Barriers You Might Have to Social Success**

We know from our experience as social coaches that everyone is "friend-able." Sometimes you might just need a little support or advice to make that happen. This book builds on the tips that we talked about in our book for younger kids, *How to Make & Keep Friends: Tips for Kids to Overcome 50 Common Social Challenges*. You can find it at the end of this book. If you are a tween, the end of our first book and the beginning of this one will be the right combination for you.

We wrote this book as a reference guide. We did not intend for it to be read cover to cover. You might find it a little boring doing it that way! You can easily flip to the section you want to know more about and read only the parts that will be interesting and helpful to you.

We had real teens, much like you, help us with writing the tips in this book. We are always interested in your thoughts about our work and are available to answer any questions you have. If you would like to write us, you can find our contact information at the end of the book.

Donna Shea and Nadine Briggs

Section 1:
Self

1

Personal Hygiene

The first and most important rule for social success is, ***don't stink****. We mean it! Bodily changes that begin at age 10 or 11 cause an increase in odors. You will need to pay extra attention to cleanliness, especially after any physical activity. Staying clean not only prevents body odor, but it will help to prevent acne as well. Good personal hygiene is one of the easiest things you can do to gain social acceptance. At a minimum, you should:*

1. Shower daily. Top to bottom. With soap.

2. It might sound like a no-brainer or even gross for us to point it out, but make sure that you practice good hygiene after using the bathroom, and leave it clean for the next person. Flushable wipes are handy to have and make cleanliness easy. Always wash your hands after visiting the bathroom.

3. Use a good facial scrub in the morning and before bed to help prevent acne.

4. Apply acne cream to your face if you have acne. Make sure that you follow the directions because overusing it can dry your skin out and cause it to peel. Acne products can make your skin more sensitive, especially if you are fair-skinned, so wear sunscreen if you use them. Be careful that these products don't stain your clothes. You might want to get dressed first, and then apply acne products to your face. If over-the-counter products are not working well, see your doctor who might dispense prescription medication for you.

5. Apply deodorant with an antiperspirant every single morning and after you exercise or shower. Deodorant will help control any smell and antiperspirant will help prevent dampness under your arms. Carry a travel size one in your purse, backpack, or gym bag.

6. Wear clean clothes. An article of clothing that has been worn more than twice without washing will begin to smell, even your favorite hoodie!

7. Shampoo your hair and use conditioner (only if your hair needs extra conditioning). Comb or brush your hair every morning and night and as needed during the day.

8. Brush and floss your teeth twice a day. Even if you don't floss, you should always brush. Some people dislike brushing their teeth, but getting a cavity filled feels much worse than brushing your teeth.

9. Use mouthwash if you tend to have bad breath. Vigorously swish the mouthwash throughout your mouth for 60 seconds. Carry gum or mints for any fresh-breath emergencies!

10. Take it easy on the fragrance products. A little can go a long way. If the smell of your perfume or cologne lingers once you have left a room, then you are wearing too much. Too much fragrance can be just as off-putting to other people as body odor.

Ya know what I do every day? I wash. Personal hygiene is part of the package with me. - Jim Carrey

2

Sleeping and Eating Habits

School schedules are not kind to a teen's desired sleeping habits. Some teens have a body clock that prefers to stay up late and sleep late. Many schools start the school day at 7:30 AM, some even earlier. These early hours can make for a difficult start to the day. People who are sleep deprived can be irritable and unpleasant to be around, as can hungry people. Many teens also develop poor eating habits due to irregular schedules, busy days filled with after school activities or that natural teenage love for junk food.

1. Aim for a goal of eight to ten hours of sleep each night. If you need to be up to shower and get ready for school at 6:00 AM, lights out should be at 10:00 PM. For most people, it can take ten to twenty minutes to fall asleep at night. If it always takes you more or less time than that, you might want to make additional adjustments to help your body clock. A routine of going to sleep and waking up at consistent times each night and morning is ideal, even on the weekends.

2. Organize your schedule so that you can participate in the activities you enjoy and still get your homework done by a reasonable hour. If you are tired a lot, you might find that you are involved in too many activities and need to prioritize things in your schedule to allow you to get enough rest.

3. There are apps that can measure the quality and quantity of your sleep and even wake you up at a time when your body is in lighter sleep rather than from a deep sleep. It might be interesting to find out what your sleep quality is like and try different strategies to improve your sleep.

4. As difficult as it is, try to stay off any electronics at least 60 minutes before going to bed. Put electronics in *do not disturb* mode to stop notifications while you are

trying to sleep. It might help to put your phone on its charger in a different room and to create an auto away message for any texts that come in. Here is a link to an article for you on this topic: http://www.cbsnews.com/news/electronic-devices-may-keep-teens-from-sleeping/

5. Listen to some relaxing music. Take a bath, which has the bonus of saving you that shower time in the morning! Read a book, or enjoy another quiet, non-electronic activity to help your brain and body prepare for sleep.

6. Don't skip breakfast. Eat something every morning before going to school, something that contains protein that will stay in your stomach. Don't allow yourself to be "hangry" and irritable with people due to hunger or lowered blood sugar.

7. For the same reason, don't skip lunch. If you don't like what the cafeteria offers for choices, pack things that you do like to eat the night before and bring your lunch to school.

8. Have dinner with your family, or have a pizza and game night if everyone has busy schedules, as often as possible. Although we know many teens disapprove of forced family time, it is a great way to socially connect with the people at home and also a good way to practice conversation and other social skills.

9. Almost every teen enjoys junk food. It is part of being a teen. Try to make it a goal to eat 80% healthy foods, like proteins, fruits, and vegetables, and 20% junk food to both keep your body healthy and your mood happy. Avoid caffeinated drinks in the afternoon and evening so that they won't keep you from falling asleep later. Avoid too much junk food as it can aggravate any skin problems you may have.

10. Good eating habits also include good table manners. Make sure that you chew with your mouth closed, wipe your mouth with a napkin, burp as quietly as possible, and use utensils properly.

If people were meant to pop out of bed, we'd all sleep in toasters. - Unknown

3

Personal Power

Do you have times when you feel anything but powerful or confident? Do you feel overwhelmed by the demands put on you? A sense of personal power can help increase your self-esteem. Find ways to fight back against insecurity and your teen years will be much easier.

1. Even if you struggle with feeling unhappy about some aspects of yourself, it is never acceptable for anyone to act in a disrespectful manner towards you. On the flip side, people who are not feeling good about themselves might take that out on other people around them. Treat other people the way you wish to have them treat you in return.

2. **Only _you_ have the power to change the parts of your life that you are not bringing you happiness**. Your parents, teachers, or coaches, cannot do it for you, although they are great people to ask for advice. Yes, it can be hard to make changes, but you can do it.

3. If you feel that the rules at home are unfair, take steps to change things by talking about it with your parents. Think about it ahead of time and come up with new rules for your parents to consider. It might be helpful to write it out. Calmly and maturely, with no anger or disgust in your voice, discuss the possibility of changing the rules with your parents. For example, a reasonable rule to change might be to ask for a later curfew if you still have the same one that you have had for a while. Keep in mind that your parents might not agree with you, but if you approach them in a reasonable and adult-like fashion, you might be able to find a compromise. If they do not agree, ask if there are steps they would like to see you take to be able to make a future change in a rule.

4. If you have an issue with an adult who is not your parent, calmly ask them to help you understand the issue. Try not to accuse, question the adult's authority, or tell them that their view is wrong, especially if you are upset. You might say, "Can you help me understand why?" If you approach an issue from the standpoint of a learning experience, you will make that adult more likely to listen to what you say.

5. You might feel powerless if someone you know is teasing or pranking you and thinks what they are doing is funny. The way you react has much to do with your relationship with that person. If it is someone that you don't know very well, your best bet is to ignore it or shrug it off. A strong reaction might encourage the person to do it more. Even if it is annoying you, try not to make it into a big deal. Pay attention to your tone of voice and body language, so your whole body shows that it does not bother you. Keep in mind that it is okay to feel upset, but try not to show it at that moment. If you think that the issue needs an adult to intervene, wait until you have a private moment to talk to a trusted adult about how to handle it. On the other hand, if the teasing is from a good friend you will need to respond differently. You might try to laugh it off. If it persists and it is still bothering you, firmly, but nicely and without yelling, tell your friend, face-to-face, "Look, I know you're just messing around, but I don't like that, and I want it to stop."

6. Are you a teen who spends a lot of time home alone on the weekends and during vacation weeks waiting for the phone to ring? Take control. Send out a text or two and plan something to do with friends. To save face in the event no one responds, you can be vague when you ask. Try saying, "Anyone around this weekend to see a movie or something?"

7. There is personal power to be gained in making changes based on feedback. If someone has given you feedback, for example calling you annoying or roasting you, consider the reasons why they might say these things about you. If you ask that person what they meant, they might not tell you to spare your feelings. They might believe that you should know already. Think of someone you could ask who would be honest with you. Your school counselor can be a good, impartial person. We all have character traits that bear noticing, and we can improve. It might not be easy to hear, but it's helpful to know.

8. Adults in your life do not want you to hurt yourself by abusing drugs or alcohol. However, if you are ever under the influence of drugs or alcohol and you have lost control, ask a trusted sober friend to bring you home, or call your parents even if you think they will be angry and discipline you. You can tell your parents, "I can't drive right now. Could you please pick me up? We can discuss my choices in the morning." Don't stay somewhere if you are not feeling in control of yourself. Don't drive. Safety comes first. Personal thinks you are annoying, but it is helpful. It is better to understand and work on improving your interactions with others than to be excluded from fun activities and parties only because you do not understand the impact your actions have on those around you.

9. When you are in a friendship or dating someone, make sure you are not spending your time with someone who tries to dominate or control you, either physically or emotionally. It truly is better and safer to be without friends or a significant other temporarily than to be with someone who treats you badly.

10. When dating or hanging out with someone who is interested in you romantically, remember that, when it comes to physical or intimate actions, "No means no."

Even if the person previously said yes, you must still stop. It is vital for you to remember; **no means no,** and if a person does not stop, they are breaking the law. Personal power comes from the ability to know yourself, to know what is best for you, to make good choices on your own, and to know how to stay safe even when you have made some choices that are not good for you.

Don't put the key to your happiness in someone else's pocket; keep it in your own. - Unknown

4

Optimism

Some people are just naturally optimistic in how they react to life events. Others take the opposite view. If you tend to look at the negative side of things, we have good news. There are simple exercises you can do to become a more optimistic thinker. A well-known psychologist out of Penn State, Martin Seligman, created a movement known as positive psychology. Dr. Seligman researched optimism, and he shares his exciting findings in his many books on the topic. For more about his research, visit http://ppc.sas.upenn.edu/research/positive-psychology-research or read some of his many books. His research has shown that, when people focus on the positive aspects of their lives, they begin to feel more resilient and optimistic. Some of the tips here are from his findings.

1. Simple exercises and shifts in thinking can make a significant difference in how you look at the events in your life. You have total control over how you handle the good and the bad that happens during your teen years. And there will be both. You have the power to make a change in how and what you think.

2. The more you think about the positive aspects of your life, the more your brain will be open to those positive thoughts. Remember a particularly happy time. Think about that memory for a while. Focusing on happy thoughts is a great exercise to help you think more optimistically. Try smiling more. The simple act of smiling can create more positivity in your life.

3. Keep a journal or write down three things that make you happy or for which you are grateful and why, either each day or once a week (if daily feels like too much). Focusing on gratitude is another great way to increase your optimism. Try this exercise for at least a few

weeks. Rate your daily happiness on a scale of 1 to 10 in your journal. See if the number goes up by focusing on the good stuff.

4. When you have a setback, failure, or a bad day, think of what you might have done differently and listen carefully to the self-talk going on in your mind. Try not to be too hard on yourself. Everyone has an occasional difficult day. Work on how to prevent future bad situations from happening instead of thinking about or talking about how bad you felt. Guilt keeps you stuck. Limit your regrets to a brief period and then use your time to move forward by developing a plan for change. Shift your thoughts toward problem-solving rather than staying stuck on what went wrong. A great thought to keep in mind is that, for every problem, there is a solution.

5. Create a poster or vision board of your dreams or things you enjoy. Keep it in view where you can look at it frequently. Hang it on your bedroom door, the fridge, or a wall in your room. A visual will remind you that you enjoy many things in life and that you have big dreams to chase! Imagine yourself living that dream and revel in how amazing you will feel when it comes true. Notice how we said, "when it comes true" and not "if it comes true"? Framing your thoughts in a positive manner primes your brain to be more resilient.

6. Create positivity for someone else by volunteering your time to help others. There are many ways that teens can contribute their time and talents. Helping someone else is a known and proven way to boost your outlook. Some ways that you can help others include:
    a. Volunteer at a senior center, food pantry, animal shelter, library, hospital, etc.;
    b. Help an elderly neighbor with their lawn care by mowing, raking leaves, spreading mulch,

shoveling snow, or whatever they need. Do this to be kind to that person without any expectation of payment.

7. If you know that someone is going through a particularly tough time, ask if there is a way for you to help. For example, carry the backpack for a classmate on crutches. Hug your parent. We know a teen who organized a social media funding campaign to provide warm blankets, socks, hats, and gift cards for coffee to a local homeless shelter.

8. Random acts of kindness also boost optimism. Try holding doors open for people, pay for the order for the person behind you in line, or make a small donation to a fundraiser. Bring some homemade cookies to the local police or fire station. Visiting community helpers might feel a little less weird if you call them first to let them know you are coming. You could even organize a couple of friends to do it with or make it part of a larger group effort. For more ideas, visit https://www.randomactsofkindness.org/kindness-ideas.

9. To get a huge optimism boost, try a *gratitude visit,* as described in the book *Flourish* by Martin Seligman. The gratitude visit is said to result in less depression and greater happiness for an entire month. This exercise involves thinking of someone for whom you are grateful and then writing down around 300 words about why. The letter should be specific about how this person makes your life better. Then schedule an uninterrupted time to sit with them and read the letter to that person. Ask them not to interrupt as you read how much they mean to you, have helped you, or why you are grateful for that person.

10. Make time to sit quietly and evaluate your life. Think of any of aspects of your life that you would like to change. Many teens get caught up in thoughts of

sadness or anxiety that they feel are impossible to fix. Form a plan to reduce the things that are negative in your life, such as keeping your room clean so that you can find your stuff, dropping an activity that doesn't bring you joy anymore, or releasing yourself from a toxic friendship. But don't stop there. The next step is to think of active ways to increase the positive aspects of your life too!

Optimism is a happiness magnet. If you stay positive, good things and good people will be drawn to you.

 - Mary Lou Retton

5

Standing Your Ground

Sometimes teens are jerks to other teens. Sometimes parents, teachers, and coaches are unfair. You might find that there are groups that you want to join but the other people in the group want you to act in a way that you do not like. It can be hard to do, but standing your ground about issues and values that are important to you is more of a priority than what other people think of you.

1. It is important to find a way to stand your ground that feels comfortable to you. Find a way to express yourself in your personal style about things that matter to you to prevent people from thinking they can control you or take advantage of you. As you consider your style, think of someone you know that you have seen hold their ground and how they went about it. Instead of copying how they do it, borrow some of what you liked and make it your own.

2. Self-assured people handle standing their ground with confidence. They stand tall and face the other person eye to eye and state their case without pausing or stumbling over words a lot.

3. The choices you make are a step toward taking control of some aspects of your life. It is also a way to increase your personal power or self-esteem. You might find that, as you practice standing your ground, your confidence improves.

4. If someone does or says something you do not like, you can try to brush it off with a joke and then change the subject to something else.

5. If someone is pressuring you, offer a reason why you don't want to participate. For example, you could say,

"If my coach caught me doing that, I'd get thrown off the team!" or, "Are you trying to get me grounded or something?"

6. If you feel that your parents treat you unfairly, have a mature discussion with them about it and see if you can find a compromise.

7. Even though it might be hard if you are in a position of having to stand your ground, you need to remember that getting heated or angry won't help the situation. If you are having trouble with this, you can take a break and approach the person after you have a chance to calm down. Taking a break will also give you more time to consider what you are going to say.

8. If possible and reasonable, just remove yourself from the situation. That might be signal enough that you will not be part of whatever is going on.

9. If it is a minor thing, it is okay to pretend you did not hear it and just ignore it. Keep your facial expression blank, and body language relaxed. Relaxed body language is when your shoulders are down, and your hands are in your pockets.

10. If you have real friends who are with you at the time, ask them to back you up and hold your ground despite the pressure. Unfortunately, you might find that your true friends will also try to pressure you. If they do this, it does not mean that they are not your friends anymore, but you will still have to stand your ground.

Even with them. You might need to say, "Hey guys, back me up next time. When you take their side, it's not helpful!" Don't shout, but say it with a strong voice. The consequences you would face by giving in to peer pressure are just not worth it.

It's better to walk alone than with a crowd going in the wrong direction. Do what you feel is right. - Diane Grant

6
Building Self-Confidence

Wouldn't it be great to feel confident when socializing? Or even all the time? It is probably no surprise to know that research shows confident teens are much less likely to be the target of bullying. Self-confidence is an inner strength that other people can sense. It is an understanding and acceptance of yourself and who you are as a person. Check out these tips and traits that confident people use and have. You can use them to build your confidence "muscles."

1. Develop the outward physical signs of confidence. These include standing up straight and tall and looking relaxed. If you gently cross your arms or lightly place your hands in your pockets, you will look more relaxed. If you feel tight, roll your shoulders. Look people in the eye but, if this is difficult for you, keep your head up and focus your eyes just above the other person's eyes. Try not to look down. Practice self-confidence daily when you are alone. Stand in front of a mirror and check out your posture as well as your facial expression. It will help you understand how others see you when you are talking to them.

2. There are verbal traits that self-confident people demonstrate along with their body language. When you are speaking, use a clear and strong voice. Avoid being too loud or too quiet or, even mumbling. Sometimes, when teens are uncomfortable, they use a different voice than the one they normally use. Speak in your real voice.

3. Confident people are adept at handling embarrassing moments. Remember that everyone has experienced embarrassing moments and has lived through them! The best thing to do is not to make a big deal about it. If no one says anything, just be quiet and let it go. Or

you can laugh it off. Don't be afraid to make fun of yourself.

4. If the voice inside your head is negative, shift your thoughts to a more positive and helpful voice. Don't allow your internal thoughts to bully you. Write down a list of things that are good about yourself and read it when you are feeling insecure. Practice this, and you will find that you can shift your thoughts more easily.

5. Confident people know when to ignore what other people think or say. If someone is putting you down because they are jealous of you, that is a good thing to ignore! Confident people also know when to listen to and consider important feedback given to them. If a friend tells you about something you are doing that is bugging them, pay attention to what they say. Be careful not to confuse confidence with arrogance. Confidence will attract other people to you, but if you act in an arrogant, snobbish, or know-it-all manner, you will drive other people away.

6. Build your self-confidence by finding out what your strengths are and what you are good at doing. Try out different activities to see what fits you well. You might not know that you are a good writer, that you can sew great fashions yourself, can create videos or graphic art, or even play the piano or hockey. The list of what people, including you, can be good at is endless.

7. In the same way that volunteering for a good cause can create positive feelings, you will boost your self-confidence as you help other people. The act of helping can make you feel valued and needed.

8. Are you shy or do you have trouble speaking up in class? Try being more social by participating in a school play or local theater production. Take a public

speaking class to help build your vocal confidence. Try sitting in the front of the room, so if you do talk in class, you will not have to see everyone looking at you.

9. Confident people are not afraid to ask questions if they are unsure of what to do. If you are confused about a situation or think that you might not have heard a question correctly, ask for clarification. An effective way to do that is to repeat the question back or express the situation in your words to see if you understood it correctly.

10. The thing to remember about building self-confidence is that you can fake it 'til you make it! You can even fake it until you *are* it. Did you know that even many adults do this? Even if you don't feel a whole lot of confidence yet, every time you practice standing tall or keeping your head up, it eventually becomes part of the confident self that you present to the world. You may want to check out Amy Cuddy's Ted Talk about power poses. She studied how to increase feeling powerful and confident by holding a power pose for only two minutes. It's worth watching the entire talk. Here is the link: https://www.ted.com/talks/amy_cuddy_your_body_language_shapes_who_you_are.

Never say anything about yourself you don't want to come true. - Brian Tracy

7

Defend and Deflect

All of us have been on the receiving end of mean remarks or had our feelings hurt at some point. Maybe a friend criticized you or left you out of an important social invitation. Maybe someone who is not a friend decided it would be funny to roast or insult you. Knowing how to defend and deflect is one of the most important social lessons. It is a key way to prevent more negativity from coming your way.

1. If you get upset and feel the need to defend yourself, take a second to consider if you are reading the other person's intent correctly. You wouldn't want to vehemently defend yourself if you misunderstood what the other person meant.

2. You always have the right to feel what you feel. We are not saying to suppress the feeling, but to work on concealing a strong reaction. Despite how upset or angry you feel at that moment, and rightfully so, try not to let your body language, your facial expression, or your voice react in a big way.

3. If you are not skilled at putting an "I don't care" expression on your face, practice in a mirror at home. Your expression cannot show your true feelings, or you will give evidence to the person who wants to upset you that they have succeeded. You truly need to appear as though you don't care. Dealing with someone intentionally trying to upset you is one case when you need to be boring. It is necessary to mask your true feelings so that the other person will move on.

4. If you slump your shoulders, look down, or withdraw into your body, you are also giving the person who is bothering you proof that they have upset you.

5. If you are a naturally funny person, use that humor to express that the other person's actions don't bother you, even if they do. If you can make a joke and laugh it off, you are demonstrating that the other person cannot get to you.

6. However, if the person is a real friend of yours, you might handle the situation differently. You can be much more direct with a friend by saying, "Dude, chill!" or, "What was up with that?" While we understand that you don't want to hurt your friend, how your friend responds is less important than the fact that you are calling them out on the thing they did to upset you. Hopefully, your friend will apologize to you. If your friend was having a mean moment, they might try to come up with some excuse for their actions that you probably will not believe. Even if your friend becomes defensive when you talk to them, you should stand your ground and tell them how you feel about the way they treated you. You could say, "We're still friends, but I just want you to know how I felt, whether you see it that way or not."

7. If you are frequently defending yourself against a friend, you might need to decide if you want to continue to hang out with them. Friends are valuable, so deciding whether to snip someone out of your life or not is a huge deal. You should forgive small infractions so that the friendship remains intact. However, if the breach was significant, or if there are multiple ongoing problems in the friendship, then you must consider whether you want to continue the relationship.

8. If you decide to pull back from a friendship, be discreet and don't announce that the friendship is over. When you say that to someone, you can cause hurt feelings

and maybe even backlash. Leave open the option to re-visit the friendship, should you change your mind in the future. Most people pull back by not calling or texting as much and being politely unavailable to accept a friend's invitations. People can and do change, so don't abruptly cut the friendship ties completely.

9. If you do decide to continue the friendship with the person, it might be necessary to let them know that it is not okay with you if they treat you in that way again. You might need to stand your ground, and set limits. We suggest communicating this in a non-aggressive way, such as, "We're all done with that stuff that went on, right? Because I was not okay with it."

10. Remember that temporarily being without friends is a better and healthier option than having friends who treat you badly or get you into uncomfortable situations. Real friends are out there. Don't waste your time with people who treat you poorly.

When someone disrespects you, beware the impulse to win their respect. For disrespect isn't a valuation of your worth, but a signal of their character. - Brendon Burchard

8

Mistakes and Apologies

Everyone makes mistakes. A person who owns up to their mistakes scores likeability and trust points. There are times in life when you should offer an apology. There are also times in life when an apology needs to be accepted.

1. Offering a sincere apology to someone is certainly not an easy thing to do. It is admitting that you made a mistake, so it is not something that anyone likes to do. As you get older and more mature, it is necessary to maintain relationships that you have developed over the years. It is not worth losing a relationship because of how difficult it is to apologize.

2. Before apologizing, the other person needs to be ready to receive an apology. You will need to read both the situation and the person to determine if they are willing to hear your apology. Sometimes people need a cooling off period before they are emotionally ready to hear an apology. If the individual is not ready to be around you or gives you the cold shoulder by ignoring you, they are not ready. Even though you might want things resolved right away, don't try to apologize to someone who is not willing to accept it.

3. An apology has three parts to it:

   a. You need to be genuinely sorry to give a meaningful apology.

   b. Tell the person you are sorry once, not repeatedly, and specifically say what you are sorry for, to avoid any confusion.

   c. Make a concerted effort not to let the same mistake for which you are apologizing happen again.

Here is a sample apology if you told a friend's secret to someone else, and your friend found out:

You need to be genuinely sorry for telling the secret and not just sorry that you got caught.

"I'm sorry that I told Amanda that you liked Justin. I really shouldn't have told something so personal, especially after I promised you that I wouldn't. I hope you will still trust me, but I understand that you might not. I hope to gain back your trust someday."

4. Avoid the rapid-fire, "Sorry, sorry, sorry." A person may lose the feeling that you are genuinely remorseful when the word "sorry" is repeatedly delivered in this way. We also see people who use this method of apologizing just to avoid the issue at hand. An apology that is not backed up by an actual change is entirely meaningless.

5. If you are a person frequently finds yourself In a position of needing to apologize, do some self-reflection about why that is. You might need to work on impulse control. Perhaps you need to stop and think before speaking or doing things so that you don't say or do things that require an apology. Consider taking a slight pause to run your thought through the T.H.I.N.K. method (creator unknown) before you say it out loud. Is what you are about to say:

      a. True?

      b. Helpful?

      c. Inspiring?

      d. Necessary?

      e. Kind?

If not, it is likely better left unsaid.

To stop yourself from doing impulsive things, try to implement the strategy of, "Ask before action." For example, before eating some cookies that you see in your kitchen, ask your mom, "Is it okay if I help myself to a couple of cookies?" That way, if she was making them for a party or bake sale, she won't get mad.

6. When someone tells you a secret, it might seem like you absolutely must tell someone else, or you will burst. If you feel this way, think about the consequences of your actions if you do tell. Think of yourself as a vault; once information goes in, it never comes out. Your friends will start to see you as trustworthy. They might even share more of their personal thoughts with you. The only exception to this rule is if your friend is telling you a secret that involves them getting hurt or in danger of being harmed, either at their own or someone else's hand. In this case, telling their secret may be the only way to get them the help they need.

7. Admitting to a mistake takes a lot of courage, especially if you know that the consequences will be fierce. Even if you don't feel bad for the mistake you made, you should try to make it right. You deserve to hold yourself to a high standard of integrity.

8. If the mistake you made is of a legal nature, for example, plagiarizing a report or violating copyright by sharing something you shouldn't have, find a trusted adult to talk to about your mistake. Trying to cover up a legal issue could result in more difficulties than you can imagine. Adults can help you to solve these significant problems.

9. Be prepared to accept the consequence of your mistake if it results in a reprimand by an adult or authority figure. For example, if your school gives you detention, serve your time with maturity rather than complaining about the detention. Remember, the adults around you are the

ones who, in the future, will write letters of recommendation for you. You want them to think highly of you.

10. It might not seem like it at first but, in the end, it will always feel better to do the right thing and accept the consequences of your actions. Having high integrity and expectations of yourself will sculpt you into a responsible young man or woman.

An apology is the superglue of life. It can repair just about anything. - Lynn Johnston

9

Filtering Your Words

If you are a teen who has difficulty with impulse control, you might tend to say whatever is on your mind, without filtering your words first. Sometimes this causes people to avoid you; the constant chatter simply wears them out.

1. Some people's minds are always on, and their thoughts can move from one topic or idea to another very quickly. Teens who are particularly curious might have more thoughts racing through their heads than those who are less curious.

2. Thinking a lot of different thoughts isn't a problem unless you speak all of those thoughts aloud.

3. Even if you think your ideas are interesting, no one wants to hear everything that you're thinking. It can become quickly annoying to your listener if you frequently interrupt them to get your thoughts out.

4. If you have a topic that you love to talk about, try to assess how much the other person likes that topic. From this, you can gauge how much you should talk about it. For example, you might love motorcycles and know everything about every make and model and the pros and cons of each bike. If the person you are talking to likes them a little, then only talk about motorcycles a little bit. If they are a huge fan just like you, then you can chat as much as you like. Be sure to give the other person a chance to add to the conversation too.

5. Even if you find someone who is as interested as you are in a topic, don't try to one-up them or prove to them that you know more or that your opinions are somehow better than theirs. If you do this, you might end up alienating the other person who shares your interest.

Instead, listen to the other person. You might be able to learn something new about your favorite topic.

6. Avoid trying to convert people into liking your favorite subject. You can ask if they are interested in learning more, but try not to push if they don't seem interested. They either like it, or they don't.

7. In your mind, freeze your thought before you give it a voice and make sure that the thought:
    a. is on-topic to what others are saying;
    b. isn't offensive to the other person;
    c. isn't related to money, religion, or politics;
    d. won't sound odd to those around you;
    e. is funny if you are attempting to be funny. Think before you say it. Consider how it will land and if you will be embarrassed if others don't find it funny;
    f. will not make you appear to be a know-it-all; and,
    g. isn't controversial unless you are looking to debate the topic. Proceed with caution here. You could severely damage friendships by bringing up controversial topics that cause major disagreements.

8. Pay attention to the feedback you get from your peers. This feedback will come to you either verbally or nonverbally. For example, if someone tells you to stop talking, then you should stop talking. If someone starts to look bored (by looking away, yawning, playing with their phone or trying to move away), then you should also stop talking or switch the topic to something the other person likes.

9. If you are with someone else who is not filtering their thoughts well or constantly interrupts you, you can try to help them by saying, "Not to change the subject, but...," or, "Let's chat about something else now," or,

"That's not my thing." It is important to give a friend time and space to talk about things they like, but it does not have to be the entire conversation every time you are with that friend.

10. If filtering your thoughts is an area you struggle with, try not to be hard on yourself. Many people have trouble with this skill and need to practice becoming better at knowing how. You will figure it out with practice. If you do happen to catch yourself interjecting an unrelated topic into a conversation, you can be a little self-deprecating and say, "Whoops! Well, that was random!"

Sometimes the thoughts in my head get so bored they go out for a stroll through my mouth. This is rarely a good thing. - Scott Westerfield

10

Uniqueness

Allow yourself to be your unique self. Give yourself permission to be who you are and not attempt to be a copy of someone else. You deserve to be yourself, the true you.

1. If you feel that the other kids at school do not appreciate your uniqueness, that might be true. But it might also mean that you have yet to find your people. Keep searching.

2. Everyone has talents and gifts that they are meant to share with the world. Yours are no more or less important than anyone else's. Treat yourself as an equal.

3. You might not yet have discovered your talents or what you are good at yet. We refer to this as your "awesome." Everyone has an awesome. If you feel worried because your friends or other teens seem to already be good at something, remember that you are still young and have plenty of time to try new things and discover what your talents and interests are.

4. Once you find your talent, explore ways to become better at it. In doing so, you will very likely meet other people who share the same interest. Try to find clubs, attend groups, or read magazines on the topic that interests you.

5. Even if your talents are different from those of your peers, take pride in what you are good at and own it as yours. Don't worry if it is not considered popular. If you enjoy it, that is all that matters.

6. It can take some bravery to be your true self around others, especially if they are critical of you. What others say and do won't change who you are deep inside.

Your talents and gifts are important to the world regardless of what other people might think.

8. If you are considered unique, Dr. Seuss has a quote that you should print and post in a place where you will see it on a regular basis. He said, *"Today you are You, that is truer than true. There is no one alive who is Youer than You."* Embrace your uniqueness and wear it proudly with your shoulders back and head held high.

9. If someone teases you or laughs at you for your uniqueness, try not to react strongly with anger or sadness within view of the person who is being mean. Use our tips in the **Defend and Deflect** section. Give your best "yeah, whatever" shrug to show that they can't bring you down and that you take pride in who you are.

10. If other people are harassing you because of your uniqueness, try to ignore it at first and see if stops. If it doesn't stop, talk to a trusted adult to see if they can help you address the issue for your situation. Also, see our section on **Bullying and Meanness** for additional tips.

Be yourself. Everyone else is already taken. - Oscar Wilde

11

Fitting In

Everyone wants to feel like they fit in and belong. As discussed in the previous section, you should always be proud to be uniquely you. However, you will also need to understand that there are times and situations when all of us are required to conform socially. At these times, out-of-the-ordinary behaviors or actions might cause other people to become uncomfortable around you. For example, when a teen engages in the pretend play that is more common for younger children, perhaps pretending to be an animal, some other people will become uncomfortable. Some of those people might say something to you, but most will keep their thoughts about what you are doing to themselves. Others might laugh at you, usually behind your back. If you engage in too many out-of-the-ordinary actions that cause uncomfortable thoughts in other people, it might become very hard for you to change what they think about you.

1. Understand that you have a private self and a public self. Having a private self means that there are some things you can do when you are at home, making bodily noises and picking your nose come to mind, that you should refrain from doing in public.

2. When you show your private self in public, people might have uncomfortable thoughts about you. You can avoid creating those kinds of thoughts in others by practicing social blending when it is required.

3. Physical camouflage includes practicing good personal hygiene, see the tips in the **Personal Hygiene** section, and wearing clothes that fit, are in style, and match the dress code of the activity or event to the best of your ability.

4. It is important to recognize that there are societal expectations placed on each of us. At some time on almost every day, all people find themselves in a position of needing to blend in. For example, a person wearing an evening gown or a tuxedo to a casual pool party and barbecue would be sticking out. Talking out loudly and laughing at a religious ceremony or a similar place where you are expected to be quiet would also cause a person to stick out. Sitting at a conference table at a work meeting with your feet up on the table would be breaking the rules of societal expectations.

5. When blending in is required, the best way to figure out how and what to do is by observing everyone else and by matching what is going on in the environment.

6. Another way to know if you are blending in is to ask yourself if your mom, dad, guardian or a good friend were with you, would they ask you to stop what you are doing? If you think they would, then stop.

7. Look at the expression on other people's faces to see if they are smiling nicely at you or giving you a look that isn't friendly. Individuals who are having uncomfortable thoughts about someone else will often whisper to someone else, giggle, or roll their eyes to others in the group.

8. If people say things to you like, "What are you doing?" or, "That's weird," then you are making them uncomfortable.

9. You might have a unique favorite topic or a passionate interest, such as World War history, that you enjoy talking about more than anything else. It might not always be appropriate to discuss your topic in a social setting. One way to blend in is to expand your knowledge of different subjects to talk about when

others are talking about them. Being able to converse about general topics such as current movies, sports teams, music, favorite TV shows, or social media trends can be helpful to engage in small talk and blend in.

10. The process of blending in is important to know if you care about the impression you make on other people or the thoughts other people have about you. However, we work with many teens who are very comfortable with standing out rather than blending in. You might have a unique sense of style, a different haircut that you like, or just, in general, enjoy moving against the social tide. Our reason for giving you tips on blending is for you to use them in areas of your life, such as a job, where blending in becomes socially necessary. We believe that, if you have the confidence to take your private self into public, that is always your choice. We just want you to understand what people might be thinking and, if that doesn't bother you, go forth and stand out.

Now in any social group whatever, even in a gang of thieves, we find some interest held in common, and we find a certain amount of interaction and cooperative intercourse with other groups. From these two traits, we devise a standard. - John Dewey

12

Managing Strong Feelings

Some people react to their emotions in a strong way and have emotional explosions when they are angry, frustrated, stressed, jealous, sad, or even happy. If you are one of them, people might tell you that you are overreacting to situations. These tips will help you to manage those strong feelings when they occur and to learn how to match the size of your feeling or reaction to the size of a situation.

1. Remember that everyone has feelings. Sometimes, handling strong feelings can be difficult. It can be harder to manage strong feelings in public than at home. Three deep belly breaths, counting to 10, or taking a break from the situation can help you to begin to calm down.

2. Try to gauge the size of your reaction to the situation. Are you reacting too strongly to something that is going on? Try to slow your brain down, think it through, and decide if it is a big deal or not. Most things are smaller deals than you might initially think, and most problems are solvable if you keep your cool. Try these ideas to help you calm down:

   a.   take a break;
   b.   listen to music,
   c.   go for a walk;
   d.   have something to eat;
   e.   take a nap,
   f.   draw or color; or
   g.   some other activity that you find soothing.

Then go back and look at the size of the problem again.

3. Talk about your feelings instead of acting out your feelings. If something is bugging you, say so. Explain

your issue but do not point fingers at the other person. If you are feeling sad, don't try to hide it. If you are feeling stressed, talk about the thing that is making you feel overwhelmed with someone else.

4. Make it a point to work at understanding what the other person is feeling, too. Offering an apology, shaking hands, or changing the subject can all help calm down those strong negative feelings.

5. Sometimes it is hard to stay relaxed and keep it together when you are having a strong sense of excitement. Take time to notice and ask yourself if your body movements and voice volume are too much for the situation. One way to gauge this is to observe what other people around you are doing and match your activity level and volume of your voice to theirs.

6. If you tend to worry a lot, you should remind yourself that everyone worries at times. It works best not to worry alone. Sharing your concern with someone you trust almost always helps to make it better and, many times, make it appear not to be as large a problem as you initially thought. It is the same for sad or lonely feelings. Don't keep it all inside. It isn't healthy for you to do that. If you are thinking it, you can be sure that others have had similar worries. Serious, life-threatening concerns, like thoughts of suicide, should never be kept to yourself. Reach out to a trusted adult such as your parent or your guidance counselor to help you find an expert who can help you manage strong feelings. There are doctors and counselors whose specialty is to assist with these feelings. **Call the National Suicide Prevention hotline at 1-800-273-8255. Their website is http://suicidepreventionlifeline.org/ and has an online chat available.** If you struggle with these

feelings, program the phone number into your cell right now, so you have it if you need it. Your life matters.

7. Try to write down, or journal about, why you feel so strongly. It can be a way to process those feelings. It can also help to write a letter, email, or text about what you are thinking and feeling, **but wait until you are calm, at least 24 hours and after you have reviewed it again before you decide whether you want to send it to an actual person. Keep in mind that whatever you write might be shared with others without your permission.**

8. Take responsibility for your feelings. Pay attention to how your body feels when the emotion comes on so you can develop strategies to manage it. Try to calm yourself down before the feeling becomes too big to control or too hot to handle. See our list of suggested calming strategies below. Practice them when you are calm so you can remember what to do when you feel emotional.

   a. Take a deep breath in while counting to 5, hold it in for five counts, then let it out slowly, also while counting to 5;
   b. Focus only on breath going into your lungs and out again while thinking of nothing else;
   c. Draw or listen to music to concentrate on a calming activity instead of the strong feeling;
   d. Think about a person you admire who can handle strong feelings well and copy what you think they would do;
   e. Go for a walk or some other form of exercise; or
   f. Spend time with a pet.

9. If your strong emotions happen a lot, create a signal for friends or trusted adults to use to help you recognize that they are happening. It could be as simple as a

hand motion or a phrase that is a clue to you that your emotions are beginning to get away from you.

10. Remember that feelings are just feelings. Everyone has them, and they are all okay. If very strong feelings frequently cause problems for you, it is okay to ask for and get some extra help from a parent, teacher, relative, pastor, counselor, or other people who are good listeners. It is also important to remember that you are not responsible for a **friend's** significant problems or feelings. As a teen, you cannot possibly counsel a friend who is depressed or anxious. Also, don't confuse helping a friend with making their problem your problem. The best thing that you can do is encourage your friend to talk to a trusted adult and, if you feel that friend is in danger of harming themselves, let an adult know what is going on.

Where we have strong emotions, we're liable to fool ourselves. - Carl Sagan

13

A Lack of Motivation

Some people seem to have an abundance of motivation and others struggle to get motivated. While all of us have our lazy days, people are not made to be naturally lazy. Use this tip list when you struggle with someone calling you lazy, or when you are not feeling motivated.

1. There may be various reasons that might be causing you challenges with motivation. The first step is to understand what is causing you to feel unmotivated and procrastinate. Evaluate what goes through your mind during times when it is hard to get going and write it down. Then devise a plan for how to work around these obstacles. The tips below might help you to figure out what those barriers are.

2. Physical or mental health conditions can be the top factor when you lack motivation. Depression, anxiety or any physical condition that might cause you to feel tired can all prevent you from functioning at your full self. If you think this might be the case with you, it is important to talk to your parent, guardian, and a healthcare professional.

3. Some people lose their motivation because they are afraid of failure. It could be that you have failed in the past and are afraid you will fail again. Remember that having failed in the past does not mean that you will necessarily fail if you try again. You might also be afraid to try something new for fear of failure, but you will not know if you do not try. You might just find that you enjoy it and are good at it.

4. You might be worried or concerned about what other people will say. Many teens, particularly those with ADHD, have been called lazy and criticized many

times. Some teens simply shut down and stop trying rather than allowing themselves to be open to more criticism. Advocate for yourself and let other people know that you are doing the best you can.

5. You might lack internal motivation, but can more easily get something done with external motivation. Set a goal for yourself with a reward, like using the car or getting a new video game, when you accomplish the goal. If you choose a reward that is important to you, it might provide the external boost you need to work your way through boring things.

6. You might find yourself procrastinating on tasks, chores or schoolwork that are boring, seem meaningless to you, or which you are afraid you will not be able to complete. Even as an adult, there are things we all do that don't necessarily bring a lot of self-fulfillment. Who finds taking out the trash or a math class you'll never use in life fulfilling? Try to coach yourself in small ways to overcome that procrastination. Tackle the little chore right away. Knock out the boring homework first. Encourage yourself to try your best and remember that failing at something is also a way of learning.

7. Keep this quote from youth expert Josh Shipp in mind. He said, "You have to do what you have to do so you can do what you want to do." Keep a calendar to-do list. Objectively organize and plan your tasks and activities for the week. Give yourself reminders on your phone to help keep yourself on track to accomplish those tasks and activities.

8. A lack of motivation can come from a feeling of being overwhelmed by too many things to do or even just too much clutter. It helps to break big projects down into more manageable chunks. For example, tell yourself you will just get all the dirty dishes from your room to

the dishwasher. After that, you might gather all the laundry and do that. Develop a chunking system for big school projects. Break down large projects into smaller steps written on sticky notes with deadlines for each step. Then stick them on a calendar where you can visually see what needs to get done, and when.

9. Instead of thinking, "Ugh, I don't want to do this," try to imagine the outcome instead. Envision your friends hanging out with you in a clean room. Imagine yourself turning in the school report on time and getting a good grade.

10. One of your developmental jobs as a teen is to find out what motivates *you*. You will be on the receiving end of lots of advice from teachers, school counselors, and your parents. It is important that you do some thinking for yourself too. If you like cars, explore the auto tech industry. If it's cooking you enjoy, apply for a summer job at a restaurant. If dancing is what you love, sign up for a class. Academics are important, but so is finding what motivates you and feeds your brain a dose of fulfillment. Then use that satisfaction to help yourself get through the chores that you find more challenging or less satisfying.

Lack of direction, not lack of time, is the problem. We all have twenty-four hour days. - Zig Ziglar

Section 2:
Others

14

The Ice Cream Social

We use ice cream as an analogy to describe the common friendship groups that form for teens and young adults. If you tend to be a literal thinker, or are not a fan of analogies, you might want to skip this chapter. We understand that these are very broad categories and that real-life people might have some, but not all, of the characteristics of one of these flavor groups. You might identify with a variety of flavors, and you might see aspects of yourself or your friends in all of them.

The Ice Cream Social groups:

Super Chunks: Example: Mocha Chocolate Chunk Peanut Butter Truffle Bomb

"Popular" kids. They tend to be good looking, good at sports, and not have significant social problems. They can act as if they are super special because of all the goodies they possess. They can be unpredictable at times. Sometimes they are too rich and too sweet. On occasion, they are too much of a good thing.

Deliciously Dependable: Example: Vanilla, Chocolate, Strawberry

Single flavor. The middle of the road kids. Nothing apparently outstanding about them. They are not gross, but no one goes crazy for them, either. Take it or leave it. Sometimes ignored, but always dependable and you know what you are getting.

Distinctively Different: Example: Peach Pistachio Coconut Raisin Swirl

Unique and different. Lots of nuts. Not very popular. Usually looked down on by the Super Chunk flavors. They don't typically mix well with others, but can sometimes blend with Deliciously Dependables. Interesting enough to try but may not want on a regular basis. Their uniqueness has yet to be appreciated.

1. Looking at groups this way can help you understand the dynamics between the social groups for teenagers and how they mix or don't mix.

2. Sometimes, the Distinctively Different or the Deliciously Dependable will do whatever they can to be able to hang with Super Chunks. They don't necessarily see the Super Chunks as loyal friends; they just want to be with the popular crowd too.

3. Popularity isn't always a good thing, and it is sometimes not even good for Super Chunks. Often, although not always, they engage in risky behaviors and feel forced to do things that they wouldn't otherwise do in to maintain their status. Peer pressure can be a big problem for the Super Chunks.

4. Super Chunks may also be with other Super Chunks only because they share the status of being a Super Chunk. Strip away all the popularity, and you find that many of them would not choose to be friends. Their friendships might not always be close and might stay on a more superficial level.

5. Distinctively Different or Deliciously Dependable teens tend to have a smaller group of friends, but those friends are authentic. These groups usually don't pressure the members to be something they are not.

6. Distinctively Different and Deliciously Dependable teens respect one another for their differences and even embrace them. Their uniqueness is celebrated rather than ridiculed.

7. Super Chunks may try to feel even more "super" by belittling Distinctively Different or Deliciously Dependables. They might try to elevate themselves at the expense of others. You might see them pointing and laughing at kids who have disabilities. Think for a moment. Do you *want* to be friends with people who would do that?

8. You deserve to be with friends who appreciate you for being you and like you because of your differences, not despite them.

9. You might see a Deliciously Dependable try on some hot fudge sauce and nuts and saunter on over to the Super Chunks to see if the group will accept them now that they are "super chunked up" a bit. It never hurts to try something new. You might see that your newly super chunked up Deliciously Dependable friend finds themselves excluded from a new group. We suggest that you gently bring them back and tell them that it is okay to lose the hot fudge and nuts because you like them just the way they are.

10. Although it may not typically happen, you might sometimes even see a Super Chunk head over to the Distinctively Differents or Deliciously Dependables to see if those groups would take them in. Even Super Chunks can feel a lot of pressure and insecurities. It is important to remember that everyone has positive and negative aspects, whatever flavor they are.

I don't mind your odd behavior. It's the very thing I savor. If you were an ice cream flavor, you would be my favorite one. - Mindy Gledhill

15
Real Friends Checklist

You don't need to have a lot of friends to be happy. A couple of real friends is more important than the number of friends on your social media accounts. You shouldn't hang out with flip flop friends (see the next section for a description of flip-flop friends) just to have company. We encourage you to work at having two good friendships in your life, in case one friend moves away, or one of your friends is busy or unavailable when you feel the need for a friend. When you do encounter a potential new friend, you can tell if they are going to be a good friend and worth your time by using these friendship test tips.

1. A good friend genuinely likes you and wants to spend time with you. A good friend usually has a lot of the same interests that you have.

2. A good friend does not want to spend time with you just to use your gaming system, swim in your pool, get you to drive them everywhere, use some other thing that is yours, or have you pay for everything.

3. A good friend does not insult you, put you down, or apply peer pressure to get you to break the rules.

4. When you are upset, a good friend will ask you if you are okay, and mean it, and ask if there is anything they can do to help.

5. A good friend accepts you for who you are and does not try to change you or encourage you to act in a different way than you normally would unless they think you are going to get yourself into trouble.

6. If you sometimes, or often, don't feel good being around a particular person, they are probably not a

good friend. However, if it is only your first or second time hanging out, feeling awkward is normal.

7. A real friend sticks up for you and always has your back. A good friend cheers your successes and does not make you feel as if you are less than anyone else.

8. A good friend is always your friend, even when other teens who aren't your friends are around, or even if you are friends with another person that some people don't like.

9. A good friend does not have to be the same age, the same grade, or in your school. Anyone can be a good friend.

10. Of course, if you want to be a good friend in return, you should do all these same things for your friends!

You don't need a certain number of friends. All you need is a number of friends you can be certain of. - Rola Mahmoud

16

Changing Friendships and
Flip Flop Friends

Changes in friendships are a normal part of maturing. You may be lucky enough to find friends who will end up being your friend for life but, for most of us, friends come and go all our lives. You may currently have flip flop friends, those who act like a friend one day and ignore you the next. Here are some ideas to help you manage changing friendships and flip flopping friends.

1. Friendships are bound to change as you grow older and become interested in other things or meet new people. This change is normal. If your interests change, you might want to have new friends who share your new interests.

2. Friends fill unique needs for each other. If a friendship ends, it might not be anyone's fault. It could simply be because of these changes in interests.

3. If a friend stops calling you to hang out or is spending time with other friends instead of you, think about whether you still enjoy the same things, It is possible you have gone in different directions. A changing relationship can be painful but try to remember that this is not usually personal.

4. If your friend is ignoring you, think back. Did you have an argument or did you perhaps say something to upset the friend? If a good friend has been distant or appears frustrated with you lately, there is a chance something happened that you might not be aware occurred. Check in with that person and ask, "Hey, are you upset with me?" or, "Are we okay?"

5. Consider the last time you got together with a friend who is flip-flopping. Did it appear the friend wanted to be there, or did they seem distracted or bored? Did they spend more time on social media than talking to you? These are signs that a friendship might be wearing out.

6. If you think a friendship might be changing or wearing itself out from the other person's side, try not contacting your friend for a little while and allow them some space. Your friend might just need a break to try out new friendships and may want to hang out with you again in the future.

7. Talk to a trusted adult, older friend, or sibling about how you are feeling about the friendship changing. Chances are the adult has been through this before and will understand, and might have some ideas to help you.

8. When you think about a changing friendship, consider if the friendship was truly a good fit for you. Some friendships continue longer than they should out of convenience, or because your parents are friends, and not because the friendship was or continues to be a real one. You deserve to have good friends who care about you. You might find that you are happier spending your time making new friends instead of always worrying about flip flop friends.

9. If you currently have some other friends, spend more time with them to develop those relationships instead of trying to revive a friendship that is not working right now.

10. If you have a close friend that has moved in a new direction, it might take you some time to find a new close friend, but it *will happen*. Remind yourself to hang

in there and to keep looking for new friendship opportunities. Keep a positive attitude and don't blame yourself. A temporary lull in friendships may be an exciting time to try out something new on your own. Sometimes people just need a little space. Don't try to force a friendship that is falling apart back together. Give the friend some breathing room and, if the friendship is meant to be, you will re-connect.

I've come to realize that the only people I need in my life are the ones who need me in theirs even when I have nothing else to offer them other than myself. - Unknown

17

Finding Friends

As we mentioned in the previous section, friendships can change a great deal for teens. Sometimes friends develop new interests, grow apart, or move away. You may find that you need to form new friendships. Here are our tips on how to meet potential new friends.

1. Start small. Try to make just one new friend and not feel as though you need to make a lot of friends all at once.

2. Remember to be friendly and be the first one to say hi to new people that you meet, or to people that you may know from a distance but want to get to know better. Also, don't be afraid to talk to people who come up to you first. Think of those people who may have acted friendly to you in the past and try to talk to them more.

3. Practice conversation skills with your family so that you are you ready to talk with other people. It is helpful for having a conversation to know a little about a broad range of topics, especially if you tend to be very passionate about one topic or activity. Keep up-to-date on what most teens are talking about such as current events, sports teams, music, and other common topics of discussion. Even if you cannot hold a lengthy conversation, you will know what people are talking about and have enough general knowledge to join conversations. This tip is for making general conversation you are in a social situation that requires you to do so. We are not suggesting that you give up your favorite topics. Those topics are great with your friends and other people who share those interests.

4. Remember to use active listening when other people are talking. People like to talk to good listeners. It is

important to think about listening to completely understand what the person is saying, rather than just to reply or interrupt with your thought or comment. It can help you to be a better listener by waiting a long and quiet beat before responding or adding your thought. Make sure the other person is finished speaking.

5. Show other people that you're friendly with your facial expression. Although it will probably feel weird, try practicing your smile in a mirror when you are alone. Just like magnets, people have energy that will attract or repel other people. A genuine smile with an open, friendly demeanor will attract people to you. Frowns, angry-looking or closed-off expressions, and looking down at the ground all give off the vibe that you aren't friendly or interested in potential friends. Other teens might decide not to approach you or talk to you if you are not giving off a friendly vibe.

6. If you must team up for a group project in school, try to work with someone you may not have thought to ask before. Try to go out of your comfort zone and approach someone new to sit with at lunch. Try saying, "I'd like to sit with you guys, thanks." You should watch and read their facial expressions to see if the group has welcomed you. When that happens, listen to the conversation and add comments if you can relate to the topic but don't take over the conversation. Go slowly and try to read how others are reacting to you. If you have a bold personality, you may want to let it out slowly with people who are just getting to know you. If the group at the table rejects your request to join them, they aren't worth your time. Hold your head up, move on, and try again with a different group.

7. When you engage in a conversation with someone new, or with someone you don't know very well, ask

what kinds of things they like to do. Try to find some interests that you have in common. Start with something you know you have in common and build from there. For example, if you are both in the same history class, you could say, "What'd you think of that test yesterday?"

8. Remember that you aren't alone and that other teens also want to make new friends. They might be just as interested in having you as a friend as you are in a possible friendship with them. Keep positive thoughts in your mind. Replace the thought, "No one will ever like me," with, "I would be an excellent friend."

9. Do you find it tough to find friends at school? Joining a club or doing volunteer work outside of school is a terrific way to meet people with similar interests and to bond with them around those interests. A bonus of volunteer work is a good feeling that comes when you help someone else out.

10. A safe way to test out a potential friendship and not leave yourself open to rejection is to throw out a feeler for a get-together first. You could ask a new person, "Do you like to swim? Maybe you could come over and hang out at our pool sometime?" or, "I've been thinking about seeing (fill in the name of a current movie). Have you seen it yet? Maybe we could find a time to go if you haven't?"

Of all the things you wear, your expression is the most important. - Janet Lane

18

Adjusting to Social Feedback

An important aspect to adapting to social feedback is being able to interpret what is going on in social situations. Accurately reading body language is an important part of adjusting to feedback. In fact, 70 percent of all communication between people is non-verbal. An individual who finds it easy to be socially successful is good at interpreting what people are saying both with and without words. They have learned how to respond and adjust themselves accordingly to both verbal and non-verbal messages.

1. When you are out in public, take the time to people watch. Just practice looking at people and their body posture, gestures, and facial expressions. Try to determine what they are *saying* without words. Does the person appear happy or frustrated? Does the other person seem interested in what someone is saying or do they look bored? Look for people who you think seem friendly or kind. Try to identify what is it about them that makes you feel that way?

2. Learn the common non-verbal signs that many people use, and watch for them. For example, someone who keeps looking at their watch or phone might be running late or growing tired of the conversation. They might need or want to stop talking with you, but they are not saying so with words. That person is saying it with their actions. Other ways that people communicate with their body language is in the way they tilt their head, whether they make eye contact or not, their overall facial expression, slumping shoulders versus shoulders that are pulled back, slouching, having their arms folded across their body or if they are turning their body away from you.

3. People who take over a conversation and only talk about themselves or their interests are hard to talk to and aren't fun to be around. If you think you tend to be that person, you may want to work on remembering to allow other people a chance to talk. It can be difficult at first to be a good active listener and to not switch the conversation back to yourself or your particular interests all the time. Paying attention to how many times you use the word "I" instead of the word "you" can help with this skill. If you only talk about yourself, you may notice that people will give you non-verbal messages of avoidance. They might continue to walk away from you while you are trying to talk to them, or they might cross their arms. They might tap their feet in an impatient way in hopes that you will change the topic or end the conversation. It is important that you watch the other person's body language. If you see any of these signs, you can throw in a topic switcher. You can say something like, "Enough on that, what have you been up to?"

4. If you have been told or know that you have difficulty maintaining personal space with people, look for feedback that you are in someone's uncomfortable zone. If a person is leaning away from you, you might be too close. Take a step back. If other people are taking a step back from you, you are too close. Don't take a step forward. If you aren't sure if you are too close, take a step back just in case.

5. The same goes if you are sitting too close, or looking over someone's shoulder. If someone is leaning or moving away, it is important to respond by creating more distance between you and that person. Looking over a shoulder to see something without being invited bothers some people. Wait for an invitation from the person to look at their tablet, phone, newspaper, or whatever else it is they are reading.

6. If someone says to you, "Stop," or, "Cut it out; that's annoying," and you aren't sure what it is you are doing that is bothering them, ask the person to identify for you what they want you to stop. Some people will not tell you. If that is the case, you might try saying, "Seriously though, I didn't mean to annoy you. What did I do that you didn't like?"

7. If you feel that someone is giving you a mean or dirty look, think about what your facial expression is showing. Consider if something just happened that may have upset or angered the other person, or caused them to have an uncomfortable thought about you. Self-reflection is an important part of responding and adjusting to social feedback.

8. If you tend to be a very literal thinker, you might find that you have more difficulty than most people interpreting the social feedback that others give you. You may struggle with accidentally angering someone when you didn't mean to do so. We worked with a teen whose teacher asked a rhetorical question (a type of question that you are not expected to answer and should not answer). In this case, the rhetorical question was, "Who do you think you are?" to which the teen responded, "I'm Susan." When the teacher then asked the student, "Are you talking back to me?" the teen replied, "Yes." because, in her mind, she was conversing with the teacher. Unfortunately, she was disciplined and was confused about why. We had to help her understand that when an adult says the words "talking back," that adult is telling you that they think that you are choosing to be disrespectful.

9. Frequently, social feedback comes in the form of sarcasm, which can also be difficult to interpret. If you're unsure if someone is deliberately being mean to you or joking with you, observe the person's face and

note the tone of voice they are speaking in to see if there is a match. Sarcasm that includes humor will usually have a snarky tone but with a friendly facial expression. People sometimes also use sarcasm to be demeaning or mean. If there is additional snarkiness with a demeaning tone, eye roll, or mean facial expression, then the sarcasm is intended to be mean. If you think the sarcasm was intended to hurt your feelings, see both our **Defend and Deflect** and **Bullying and Meanness** sections.

10. Hurtful social feedback can come when you find yourself not being included or invited to join in activities or parties. It is also crucial, and a very hard thing to do, to self-reflect and ask yourself if there is something that you are doing or saying that might cause other people to leave you out or not to invite you. Do you do some things that might seem annoying to other people? Do you sound bossy or controlling sometimes? Do you break confidences or get caught being untruthful? Do you perhaps talk over people and interrupt them as you try to converse? Maybe it isn't anything you are doing, but more something you forgot to do, such as keeping up with good personal hygiene. As hard as it is, negative social feedback can be helpful. Everyone has areas where they can grow and improve. Figuring out what those areas are for you is the first step towards improved social success.

People may not always tell you how they feel about you, but their actions will speak for themselves. Pay attention. - Ash Sweeney

19

When Others Annoy You

There will be times, probably lots of times, when other people do things that you find annoying. It is important to know how to inform other people about what is annoying you and to state the problem in a way that gets your needs met without demeaning or angering the other person.

1. Often, things that are annoying to people have some sensory component to them. You may be sensitive, among other things, to people talking too loudly, making certain noises, touching you, or standing too close. Understand your annoyance triggers. If crowds or waiting in lines bothers you, you may want to adjust your plans to go at a less busy time or purchase tickets online ahead of time.

2. It can be helpful to state the problem from your personal sensory perspective. For example, "I know I have sensitive hearing. When people speak a little softer, it helps me to listen better."

3. Sometimes your annoyance with other people may be because you might be jealous. Consider if that may be contributing to how you are feeling.

4. In a matter-of-fact and respectful manner, identify to the other person what is annoying to you. For example, "I have a tough time concentrating when there are other noises around. Could you stop humming for a bit?"

5. Yelling at the other person to stop does not usually help. It may even make the person do the thing that is annoying you even more.

6. Sometimes you may need to be the one that moves away from or provides an intervention to whatever it is

that is annoying you. Be sure to remove yourself quietly and in a mature fashion. Don't make a big deal out of removing yourself or state loudly why you are doing so.

7. Consider that you might be seeing yourself in the other person's annoying behavior. Many times, at our centers, we see teens getting annoyed with other teens for doing the same things that they do themselves.

8. If you are an easily annoyed person, and frequently complain about or express annoyance with others, you might find yourself a target for people who will try to annoy you on purpose to get a reaction. Consider whether the thing that is annoying you is something you should put energy into, or not. Practice being in environments that annoy you by yourself or with your family, so that you will better manage them when you are with peers. For example, if your friends like the mall and the noise and crowds bother you, try practicing going to the mall in small doses with just your family. If the cheering, the sound of a dribbling basketball, or other noises at school sports events are too loud for you, try it out with earplugs.

9. From time to time, everyone does something annoying or has annoying habits. In real friendships or solid relationships, you may just have to overlook the smaller annoyances for the greater good of the relationship. An example of something that you might want to deal with and ignore is if you have a friend who swears. Swearing bothers some people, while others don't see it as a problem.

10. Being exposed to, or working with, people doing annoying things is inevitable. You can't force someone to be quieter, stand further away from you, or stop whistling. You can, however, remind yourself that there are things you have control over and things you cannot

control. You may need to let it go and ignore it even if you don't want to.

That awkward moment when someone yells at you for clicking a pen, but you have to click it one more time to use it. - Unknown

20

Crushes and Flirting

Romantic relationships require an elevated level of maturity. If you still enjoy games and activities that younger kids enjoy, that is fine. There is no need to worry about these types of relationships until you feel ready, regardless of what your same-aged peers are doing.

When we refer to love interests, we are speaking in gender-neutral terms. Romantic relationships can occur between people of the opposite or the same genders and, for some people, both. Some teens are just beginning to figure out their preferences, so it is entirely okay if you aren't sure yet.

1. Interest in romantic relationships and asking people to go out typically starts toward the end of middle school, but many kids experience crushes as early as elementary school. We know that being a couple can seem exciting, but we encourage you to consider just being friends for a while before starting a more romantic relationship. Once you have reached your 18th birthday, you are considered an adult and should not date people who are not at least 18 years old.

2. The single most important rule of attraction to someone else is that you respect the boundaries of the other person and that they respect your boundaries. If someone is pressuring you to do something that you don't want to do or is controlling you in any way, don't stay with that person. The people that you are romantically involved with should never try to, or be allowed to, hurt you physically or emotionally, and should listen to you when you say "No." No means no. Every time.

3. Punching, kicking, shoving, saying demeaning things, humiliation, and other forms of physical or verbal abuse

aren't acceptable in any relationships, romantic or otherwise. This type of behavior should never be considered flirting by either of the people involved.

4. Flirting is used to show another person that you are interested in them in a romantic way. Be sure to save flirting only for the people you have a crush on or like in a romantic way. If you flirt with everyone, not only will it lose its meaning for the special people in your life, but people will think that you don't respect yourself and your body. You may end up getting a reputation based on what people believe that you are like rather than who you genuinely are as a person.

5. Flirting with someone could include:
   a. Smiling at them a lot;
   b. Letting the person catch you looking at them and then smiling;
   c. Being funny and joking around with the person, but not too much;
   d. Giving them a compliment; For example, saying something like, "I'm glad you're my lab partner" or "I love when the cute guys are in my homeroom" or "You look great when you wear that color."
   e. Touching someone lightly on the arm when you are talking to them. Just don't overdo it;
   f. Trying to sit with them or near them; and
   g. Asking the person to hang out sometime

6. As we mentioned in Tip #1 of this section, we encourage you to spend time with your crush as friends before trying to start a romantic relationship. The other person should get to know you well before you ask them out, and vice versa. Starting off as friends can help you discover your shared interests. Take your time to show the person you are interested in that you care about them. You stand a higher chance of getting

rejected if you just walk up to a crush and ask them out, without that person getting to know you first.

7. Even if you like someone a lot, only continue communicating with them in person, or on social media, if they respond to you in a positive way. If the person tells you to stop talking to or texting them, then you must stop even if you don't want to. Remember, no means no. If you continue to attempt to communicate with that person who has told you not to, they will likely become annoyed with you. If that happens, you will lose any chance of that person ever going out with you in the future.

8. No matter how attracted you are to someone else, don't stare at them. Even if the other person likes you, if you stare at them it is likely to make the person very uncomfortable, and may cause you to appear creepy. It is also imperative to be careful what you say if you are attracted to someone. Compliments are fine, but comments on more personal aspects of their body, or saying out loud what you want to do with that person, can be easily misinterpreted. We know some young people that have had to deal with sexual harassment charges for speaking very literally to members of the opposite sex. You could have sexual harassment charges brought against you for graphically describing to someone what you would like to do with them sexually, or commenting about private bodily parts to someone at work.

9. Romantic relationships should progress at a pace that is comfortable for both people. Start with hand holding and hugging before trying to kiss the other person. Never pressure the other person to engage in more than they feel ready to do. We will say it again. It is that important. No means no.

10. It can be hard when you are excited about a new relationship not to become obsessed with that person. You may feel that you want to talk to that person or be with them all the time. They will likely need to be allowed some space at times. Needing space doesn't mean that the person isn't into you, it just means that they want some time apart to get stuff done, hang out with other friends, or have some alone time. Most couples do better with a mixture of together time and alone time.

On a scale of one to ten, I'm probably a six when it comes to flirting. I'm quite shy. - Liam Payne

21

Dating and Sexuality

There does come a time, usually in your mid-teens, that biology does take over and you begin to think about, wonder about and have urges you didn't experience as a younger kid. It feels weird and exciting all at the same time. You may not even recognize at first what is going on, but you can trust us when we say that all that weirdness is very typical.

1. Don't worry; we're not going to give you a course on the mechanics of human sexuality. There are plenty of books, movies, articles, and other resources out there, as well as health classes at school, that can provide that information. Be careful though, because there is a lot of misinformation out there as well. Being embarrassed or feeling confused about all this stuff is normal.

2. Don't forget that your doctor or nurse practitioner can be a great person to answer all your questions or talk to about anything that is worrying you. It is part of their everyday job, and they have heard it all before. They won't judge you or think your questions are weird or stupid.

3. It is also quite normal to find yourself attracted to your best friend or someone of the same sex, even if you eventually do not identify as gay or bi-sexual. It is just nature trying to figure things out for you. It is usually brief and will eventually iron itself all out. You eventually figure out how you are meant to live your life.

4. If the feelings and changes that you are going through regarding sexuality create confusion as it relates to your religion or culture, you can discuss your concerns

with a trusted adult who shares similar religious or cultural beliefs.

5. Being in a serious dating or sexual relationship with someone shouldn't be taken lightly. Some teens involve themselves in "friends with benefits" situations. A casual sexual relationship is not an ideal type of relationship. You must be careful that the other person isn't just allowing casual sex just to be with you in any way they can. Many times, one of the individuals in a "friends with benefits" situation has some very genuine and hidden feelings for the other person. When this happens, this type of relationship can be very hurtful when it ends. Also, keep in mind that once you have reached your 18th birthday, you are legally considered an adult and should no longer have relationships with those under 18 years old. It is against the law for adults to have intimate relationships with those under 18 years old.

6. Never allow pressure from anyone to dictate what you do or do not do. Don't accept sexual dares from your friends. Don't let a boyfriend or girlfriend demand more than what you feel ready to give. We said it in the previous section on **Crushes and Flirting**, but if you ever hear the word "no" coming from a sexual partner, even if it is something you have done before, you MUST stop. There is a good video available that compares sexual consent to offering a person a cup of tea and will help clear up any confusion about sexual consent. You can find it here: https://www.youtube.com/watch?v=oQbei5JGiT8

7. If your interest in someone is purely physical, it is **not** going to work in the long term. Consider your motives for wanting to be with someone and their reasons for wanting to be with you. It is very easy to get caught up in a relationship. Stop and think. Nothing bad will

happen if you choose to go slow and take some time to decide about being involved in a relationship with this person.

8. Dating and serious relationships, even those newer flirtatious relationships, demand that both partners treat each other with manners and respect. You must be thoughtful, show genuine concern, and act with a special higher level of care for the other person. Little subtle gestures, such as opening doors, small thoughtful gifts, and listening to each other will mean a great deal to the success of the relationship.

9. Never share the intimate details of your relationship with your other friends or on social media even if you break up or are angry with your partner. Never pressure your partner to "sext" you (send you nude, partially nude, or sexually suggestive pictures) or share any pictures you receive from your partner. Sharing nude or partially nude photographs or having them on your mobile device is illegal.

10. Adult relationships require adult behaviors and responsibilities. If you do decide to be sexually active, you must be sure that you talk to your doctor about protecting your partner and preventing unwanted pregnancies and sexually transmitted diseases. It is vital for you to be honest and tell your doctor the truth if you are sexually active. Your doctor or nurse will keep this information confidential, but will most likely counsel you to talk to your parents, too.

I like you exactly as much as won't freak you out.

- Unknown

22

Being Excluded, Ignored, or Rejected

Every single person has faced rejection, or not being included, at some point in their life. When this happens, it hurts a great deal and is something that can be difficult to let go of or forget. Not everyone is going to be a friend, and it is important to decide when you should keep trying, stick up for yourself, or let go and move on.

1. While we would all very much like everyone to like us all the time, it is important to remember that, unfortunately, we are going to meet people who aren't nice or who treat us unfairly. It is impossible to be liked by everyone.

2. If other people are treating you in a mean or unfair manner, it is important to remember that if you let those people upset you, they will probably only do it more.

3. If other teens exclude you or don't invite you to their parties, try not to allow them to see you become upset. You can choose to let it roll off you and ignore it. You can also decide to stand up for yourself and say something like, "Wow, I don't understand why you are acting like that." We aren't telling you to ignore important feelings if you do become upset, but try not to allow the teens who are being mean to you the satisfaction of seeing you upset. If you feel sad or hurt by the acts of other people, it is perfectly okay to let those feelings out in a private or safe place, such as the restroom or with a trusted adult.

4. If you feel that you will continue to get more upset, or if you reach the point of begging other teens to let you hang out, come to their party, or join the group, it is time to walk away with your head held high. It is time to look for other friends.

5. Be careful not to get caught in the trap of asking yes-or-no questions that will get you rejected or excluded. You could say, "Hey guys, tell me what's up for the weekend," rather than asking, "Can I come too?" Better to say, "Hey, please move down a bit so I can sit here," rather than, "Can I sit with you guys?" You will experience better results by making direct statements instead of asking "yes or no" questions.

6. Some groups of teens have one person who acts as the leader. Sometimes, there are teens in a group who can see that the leader is being mean and might decide to leave the group and hang out with you. These are the actual "cool kids." If you get the impression that there are teens in the group who might be friendly towards you, approach them individually instead of as part of the group.

7. If you feel unfairly treated, and it is the first time that this has happened, consider that it could have been an honest mistake. If you feel repeatedly treated unfairly, it is time to handle it as being done on purpose. You can stick up for yourself and say, "Seriously, not cool, so stop." It sounds simple, but we see many teens forget to use the power that comes with just speaking up.

8. It can be a very hard thing to do but ask yourself if there is something that you have done or said that might cause other people to leave you out or not to invite you. Do you do some things that might seem annoying to other people? Do you sound bossy or controlling sometimes? Do you jump into the middle of groups and disrupt or interrupt what is going on?

9. You can talk to a trusted adult, and let them know that you are having a tough time finding the right group of friends. They might have some suggestions for you to try, or know of other groups of teens that have the

same interests that you have. Attempt initiating some social opportunities yourself. Take a class, try a sport, visit a museum or something else that interests you. Not only will this put you in a place that you enjoy, but it will also surround you with like-minded people and potential new friends. Try to find teens with similar interests and resist trying to be part of "popular" groups. If you've already tried and are still having difficulty, look for a social skills center near you that provides mentoring on how to make friends.

10. Just remember that, if certain people or friends don't work out, there are lots and lots of other people to be friendly with and those people don't have to be your age or at your school. Explore what other options you have in your area to socialize with people who will accept and like you just the way you are.

Everyone in some point in life have faced rejection and failure; it is part of the process to self-realization.

- Lailah Gifty Akita

23

Considering Another Point of View

Considering another's perspective can be a challenge for teens. Teen years are tricky for many reasons, and being able to look at how someone else is thinking or feeling about a situation can go a long way to help you maneuver through trouble spots. For example, if someone is angry with you, and you don't know why the other person is mad, your tendency might be to think, "I didn't do anything wrong." The tricky part is that, when teens are angry at each other, they don't usually tell the other person the reason. That means you must do your best to consider what the other person might be thinking to figure it out.

1. Considering another person's point of view requires you to think about the other person's life and how they react to things. For example, if you had a friend who is terrified of dogs, imagine what it would be like if they had to walk through a dog park. The dogs would be everywhere, many of them off their leashes, and they can run right up to your friend. Imagine that your friend can't easily get away from the dogs. How would they feel? Imagine what it would be like for them to be in that situation.

2. You can practice this skill while watching movies or TV shows. Consciously think about what the characters are going through and what it would be like to be that character.

3. If you aren't sure, ask others what they think about situations. Store this information about them in a "friendship file" in your brain as it will help you understand why that person reacts the way they do in different situations.

4. There is a saying that goes, "Put yourself (or walk) in someone else's shoes." Meaning, you should attempt

to understand or empathize with the way that another person is feeling, thinking about or viewing a situation. Sometimes we assume that someone else is thinking or feeling the same way that we do. They might not. Don't assume what others think or feel. Carefully consider that their thoughts might be different from yours.

5. It is important to remember that considering another person's point of view does not mean that you must agree with that person. There are many ways to think about things and, if someone has a different opinion than you do, it isn't necessarily wrong, just different. It can even broaden or change the way you think about something.

6. If you don't agree with someone on something, there are respectful ways to say so. One of the best tips we can give you on this is to use the words, "In my opinion." For example, if someone is talking about a band that you don't like, instead of saying, "That band sucks. I can't believe you listen to that crap," you could say, "In my opinion, their music is a little too metal for me. Who else do you listen to?"

7. Another way to be respectful of a different point of view is to say, "I can see why you might feel that way." You could also say, "I'd like you to help me understand your opinion on that" or "I'd like you to help me understand why you think that way about _____."

8. Keep in mind that being open to and respectful of other people's points of view will increase the chances of other people doing the same for you.

9. If someone is telling you their perspective, it isn't okay to say that you are bored, or look incredibly bored on purpose, even if you are.

10. If you discover that you and another person really can't understand each other's way of thinking about something, or how you each feel about something, the best thing to do is simply "agree to disagree" on that topic or subject and move on to something else.

Reality simply consists of different points of view. - Margaret Atwood

24

Conversation Skills

Conversation skills are essential so that others get to know who you are. They are also a way for you to understand better the interests of people you want to have as friends. The longer you know someone, the more in-depth the conversations tend to be.

1. Small talk is the conversation that you make when you don't know someone very well yet. The topics are superficial in nature. Some people don't feel that small talk should be necessary. You might think, "What's the point in talking about the weather? We're both apparently experiencing the same weather if we are speaking to each other." The fact of the weather being the same is very true, but it is a social norm to ease into talking with someone by making small talk. It can give you a chance to assess whether this person wants to engage in a conversation with you at all. It can also give you a little insight into their likes or dislikes. If they don't want to discuss something unimportant with you, they may not want to have a more in-depth discussion. They might not be interested in conversing in that moment at all.

2. The topics that another person wants to talk about may not be of interest you. Instead of letting them know that you are disinterested, which would be considered rude, listen politely and pretend interest in what they are saying. Pretending, in this case, doesn't mean that you are a fake person or that you are lying. You might even find that you learn something. By not considering your interests at that moment, it shows the other person that you care about them enough to hear about their interests. If someone is talking about a topic that you don't want to talk about or find boring, try to find a point

where you can change the subject to something that interests both of you.

3. If the conversation becomes quiet, it is probably time to switch topics and ask the other person a different question. You don't need to act funny or entertaining the whole time you are with someone to fill the empty spaces in conversations. It is okay to show different sides of your personality so they can see you as a multi-faceted person. Even if many topics aren't interesting to you, it would be helpful to know a little bit about everyday teen conversation topics. It is useful to learn a little about popular TV shows and music, sports teams, and current events.

4. If you switch topics too quickly, or without letting the other person know, they might not understand and may become confused. If you wish to change topics, use a topic-switching statement. For example, "This isn't on the subject, but I wanted to tell you," or, "Before I forget, I wanted to mention," could both be used to change the topic.

5. Try using a connecting statement so that the other person understands what your brain is thinking and linking in a conversation. For example, you could say, "I know that we were just talking about who has pets, and I forgot to mention that my aunt's puppy, Sam, had to go to the vet yesterday." If you just said, "Sam was sick," the other person would not know who Sam was or what had happened to him.

6. People sometimes get stuck on just talking about their favorite topic, whether it be weather, history, video games, or something else. If you are in a conversation with someone who does this, it is okay to say something like, "I'm not really in to _____, but it's cool that you like it," and then switch the topic. Be open to being polite and listening more about the other

person's interest or topic. You may learn something new.

7. Watch the other person to observe if they look bored with your topic. If the person isn't paying attention anymore, isn't looking at you, is checking their phone, or seems impatient, then it's possible that they are no longer interested.

8. Make a mental list of other topics that you can talk about so that the conversation isn't always the same. Pay attention to your friends' social media so that you can follow up in person on some of the things they are doing.

9. When someone starts a conversation with you, try to remember to find a way to relate what they are saying to your experiences. You can then comment or, if you can't relate, think of a follow up question to ask. Asking additional questions will help you to keep the conversation going longer.

10. As you get to know someone better, it is okay to begin to have deeper conversations by sharing details of your life. Imagine an information funnel where, at the small tip of the funnel, you share a little about yourself or make small talk. As you get to know the person better, you can slowly reveal more details about your life. It is off-putting for most people if you give too much information about your life at the beginning of a relationship.

A real conversation always contains an invitation. You are inviting another person to reveal himself or herself to you, to tell you who they are or what they want. - David Whyte

25

Social Drama

The teen years can be full of issues caused by social drama. Drama tends to increase during middle school. In general, the turbulent times of middle school will settle down by the time you enter high school, but that isn't always the case. The middle school years are a time of significant self-discovery when younger teens are figuring out who they are as individuals. Sometimes, teens will try power plays and use relationships and friendships as tools to get their way, or to increase their sense of self-worth.

1. Social drama is going to happen, and there is no way to avoid it. The best you can do is defend yourself as needed, and not insert yourself into the drama that does not involve you, and not create any drama yourself.

2. Social drama is not gendered specific. Both girls and guys create and get caught up in social drama.

3. If you have friends that have an issue with each other, your best bet is to remain neutral. Remind yourself that you don't own the problem, they do. If one friend is talking to you about the other, suggest that they take it up with the person they are having the trouble with, or just firmly state you aren't going to get in the middle of it and aren't going to talk behind someone's back.

4. Social drama mostly occurs when someone (Person #1), says something about someone else (Person #2) that is mean or insulting. The mean or derogatory remarks then get back to Person #2, and the drama begins. If you follow the rule of, "If you don't have anything nice to say about someone, don't say anything at all," you will have a better chance at experiencing less drama overall.

5. Breaking a confidence will escalate social drama to its highest levels. If someone tells you something in confidence, don't repeat it **unless that person is in real danger, in which case you should report it to a trusted adult.**

6. Be very careful who you confide in, especially if it is about having a crush on someone. It is the rare and faithful friend who will be able to keep your secrets just between the two of you.

7. If you know that you are not good at keeping secrets, make your friends aware of it. Let them know they probably shouldn't tell you any information they want you to keep confidential. You can make light of it and say, "Oh no! Don't tell me any secrets! You know I can't keep anything to myself!"

8. If someone tries to involve you in some social drama that includes you, tell them that you will be going straight to the source to get verification. Drama always gets created by a misunderstanding or a small thing that gets embellished or escalated into a big thing. It is better to go to the person who may or may not have said something and raise your concern with that individual directly.

9. People who start social drama might want attention. If you give them that attention and give energy to the drama, you will give those people exactly what they want.

10. Try a simple change of subject if someone attempts to get the social drama going. Stay off social media if there is a flare up, so that you are not tempted to comment. Posting comments will just add to the drama as it plays out. Your comments might become public, which makes things nearly impossible to fix if you say something you regret.

If you bring drama to my door, don't be surprised when I close it. - Sue Fitzmaurice

26

Bullying and Meanness

Bullying is a very real and serious problem and not something that you should ever keep to yourself. If you are currently in a bullying situation, it is important for you to understand that it isn't your fault. It also needs to stop right away. People who behave like bullies do it for varied reasons. Some people act like a bully because they are being bullied themselves, or are trying to feel better about themselves by making other people feel less than them. They might behave like a bully because they feel sad or just want to feel powerful. Even if you feel this way yourself, you have the power to choose not to be a bully. There is no such thing as a bad person, just a person who makes some wrong choices or bad decisions. You have the power to change your choices.

1. If you are being verbally or physically bullied, or are the target of mean behaviors, tell the person or people to stop it in a firm, strong voice. Speaking up takes courage, but it is important for you to do this if you feel safe enough to do it. Then get away from the person or people who are being mean.

2. You can help protect yourself from being bullied by using the tips in the **Fitting In** section and providing yourself a little social camouflage. Needing to blend in a bit more does not mean you should blame yourself or take responsibility for the bully's behavior. If you are the victim of bullying, there is no excuse for it to be happening to you. It is not your fault, but these are proven ways to decrease your chances of being bullied in the first place.

3. Avoid being around people who tend to be mean to other people. When making new friends, watch for comments from other people that sound like bullying,

for example, "I hate _____. He's such a jerk." Work at making friends with people who do not bully other people, and with whom you feel safe.

4. A bystander is someone who is a witness to bullying. Bystanders can do a lot to stop bullying. As a bystander, if you feel safe doing so, tell the people who are being mean to knock it off, or say, "That's not cool." Consider your friendship with the bully or mean person. Should you continue to be their friend if they are going to act this way, or would it be better to find some new friends?

5. You can also help by asking any victim of bullying if they are okay, and by keeping an eye out for them during lunch and in the halls to see if they are still getting bullied. Encourage that person to report the bullying. Offer to go with them when they report it. If the individual refuses to ask for help, and the situation doesn't stop or becomes worse, you should talk to a trusted adult yourself so that someone else is aware of what is going on.

6. When you discuss any bullying situation with a trusted adult, it isn't to be considered ratting someone out. When you report bullying, it can prevent someone from being seriously hurt or even from having suicidal thoughts or feelings.

7. Don't spread rumors about someone else even if you know them to be true. Don't forward e-mails, texts or online messages that say negative things about someone else. Avoid clubs or groups that consistently exclude other people.

8. If you feel as though you can identify yourself as engaging in bullying or mean behavior towards others, talk to a trusted adult about the feelings you get out of

bullying someone. If someone is telling you that you are a bully, zone in on why they may think that. Are you protecting yourself in some way? If someone is hurting you and if you are also the victim in a bullying situation, tell a trusted adult immediately. It is a fact that people who are victims will begin to bully other people, even though they know how bad it feels, creating a chain of pain.

9. If people think of you as a bully, the label could stick with you for a long time. Reputations can be hard to shake, and you might be thought of as a bully all the way through school if you don't make a different choice. If you want to stop being a bully, but are having a tough time figuring out how to change, ask your friends to help you. They can give you a signal or tell you to stop when they notice you are mean to someone.

10. Bullying is very serious, and in many states, is against the law, so tell a trusted adult and visit: http://www.stopbullying.gov/what-you-can-do/teens/index.html for more information.

Leave bullying to the bulls. Become human. - Unknown

27

Conflicts and Disagreements

One of the bigger keys to making and keeping friends is to be able to work out little issues before they turn into big problems. When you can show flexible thinking and good problem solving skills with peers, you will have a better chance of having successful friendships.

1. Arguments and disagreements with your friends, or in any relationship, are going to happen. At times, you might feel so confident that your view is the right one that it can be difficult or impossible for you to consider the other person's side of things. Standing by what you think at any cost might end up costing your friendships. Losing friends can be a high price to pay for wanting to be right. Learning how to resolve arguments or agree to disagree, without lots of anger or upset, can show your friends that you care enough to work it out. Being willing to consider the other side, or just accept the fact that there might be another side, can go a very long way to establishing successful relationships. Being in a conflict with someone does not have to end a friendship or relationship.

2. Working things out can be a tough thing to do. Let's admit it; we would all prefer things our way all the time! The reality of relationships and introducing other people into your life is that sometimes we need to compromise and allow the other person to have what they want or need.

3. A good method for working things out is to first listen to the other person's point of view, opinion, or idea. When listening to an opinion that you don't agree with, pay attention to your body language. Be sure that you aren't rolling your eyes, looking disgusted, or otherwise showing agitation. After your friend is finished

speaking, you can respectfully tell them your view and why you disagree. Once both sides have said what they think, see if you can compromise on a solution to the problem.

4. An easy example of how to work things out would be if you and a friend are planning to go to the movies but want to see different movies. You could flip a coin, be the one who changes to the friend's choice or agree to a double feature. As you practice being flexible with the small stuff, the big stuff will be easier to solve when it happens.

5. You may remember learning about fire prevention and "Stop, Drop and Roll" when you were a kid. You can use the same idea to prevent friendship fires from igniting.

    a. **Stop** – responding to the argument or person that is upsetting you,
    b. **Drop** – the subject, at least temporarily,
    c. **Roll** – with it by saying something like, "Maybe you're right," or, "Let's agree to disagree on this and talk about something else."

6. Sometimes it is the best idea to decide that friendship is more important than being right. Occasionally it is the right choice to be the person who is more flexible than the other person. But if a friend always wants their way, it is important for you to stick up for your ideas or thoughts, too. Be giving with your friends, but don't be a doormat and allow people to walk all over you to preserve a friendship or to keep a boyfriend or girlfriend.

7. Use the three C's of working things out: Cooperate, Collaborate, and Compromise.

8. Some phrases you can use when you are involved in solving a problem or an argument are, "How about we...?" or, "Have you considered...?" These phrases are a way to ask the other person or people to collaborate so that everyone involved in the disagreement can share ideas and brainstorm how to solve the problem.

9. Another way to prevent conflicts before they happen is by using or inferring the phrase "in my opinion" when telling people what you think. Follow your opinion with a reason so that the other person will understand why you think or feel the way you do. We see many arguments that arise because one person disagrees with something another person says, does or enjoys. An example would be putting down a TV show that your friend likes to watch. Instead of saying, "You watch THAT show? Are you kidding me?" you could instead say, "I haven't watched that one, have you seen (name another show)?"

10. Yelling or using physical aggression never solves a problem. Those types of behaviors will only serve to make things worse. If you think about it, after you are done with all the yelling, punching, or breaking stuff, there will still have the same problem you had before you did all that, and more on top of it. Of course, everyone has bad days, and everyone yells occasionally. People who are experienced problem solvers will usually skip all of that and spend their time and energy to resolve the conflict in a more productive way.

The harder the conflict, the more glorious the triumph. - Thomas Paine

28

Teens' Rights versus Parents' Rights

As you make your way through the teen years, you will find that you and your parents will disagree on a lot of topics. This section will help you understand why that is and how to manage those disagreements.

1. It is natural and normal for you to have conflicts with your parents during the teen years. These arguments, as unpleasant as they may be, show that you are maturing and beginning to develop your ideas about yourself as a person. This process allows you to be able to leave your parents when you are an adult and create a life of your own.

2. While you are still living in your parent's home, though, you will need to follow the rules that they have in place, even if you are 18 years old and officially an adult.

3. You might disagree with the rules that your parents have in place. If you do, screaming at them won't result in a change of the rule. However, if you calmly have a discussion with your parents about the rules, and offer reasonable suggestions for change, you will have a more receptive audience. It doesn't necessarily mean that they will make the change that you are requesting, but they are much more likely to listen.

4. You are likely to be much better at using electronics than your parents. In fact, they might come to you for help with smartphone and tablet issues. However, parents have a more mature understanding of online dangers. If they restrict your online use, block you from visiting certain sites, or just request that you not search for certain topics, it is because they know that you can't un-see what you have seen. They may know that you aren't ready to see all that is available on the Internet,

and they have your best interests in mind. If your parents provide and pay for your phone, they do have a right to monitor what you do on the phone, including reading texts and monitoring your content.

5. As you mature and your parents begin to lift some restrictions, it becomes your responsibility to be a smart consumer of the internet. Remember that you can't un-see things. Think back to a time when you were little, and you saw a movie or TV show that scared you and maybe even gave you nightmares. Be careful what you watch online because you can't easily remove images from your mind once you have seen them.

6. Your parents may be more concerned about your grades and academic performance than you are. They want you to have the best future possible and will remind you to stay on top of academics, particularly if you are on a path to attend college.

7. You do have the right to figure out some things on your own. If your parents are concerned about a decision you have made, gently remind them that if your decision isn't the right one, then you will learn from that and the experience will be worthwhile.

8. You don't have the right to participate in illegal behavior without consequences. You shouldn't expect your parents to get you out of trouble for any mistakes that you make.

9. Your parents aren't responsible for funding your social life or the cost of items that you want. If you have a job or earn an allowance, that money should be used for you to go out with friends or other things. Having a job also includes the bonus of making you feel more responsible and mature.

10. You do have the right to be a uniquely different person from your parents should you choose not to follow in their footsteps.

A moment of patience in a moment of anger can help us avoid a thousand moments of sorrow. - Imam Ali (A.S.)

29

Siblings

If you have a sibling or siblings, you already know that your sibling relationship can go from friendly to adversarial and then back again. You can love them and hate them all at the same time.

1. It seems that birth order can have a great deal to do with how you act with your siblings. For example, if you are the oldest, you might be or feel responsible for your younger brother(s) or sister(s). If you are in the middle, you might sometimes feel invisible. If you are the youngest, your older siblings might be jealous of you for being the baby of the family.

2. Jealously among siblings is common. Each may feel that the other has things easier, gets away with more, is smarter, better looking, better at sports, or makes friends more easily. The list could go on. The best thing to do is not try to be just like your brother or sister. Focus on being the best person that you can be. Look for your talents. If you feel pressure from your parents to be like a sibling, respectfully remind your parents that you are a different person.

3. Your family is another social system, just like school, work, or anywhere else there are people. In the family social system, we don't have the same constraints as we do for social blending in public, so our private selves are the ones that live together. There is more of a tendency to take each other for granted or to forget to treat each other with kindness and respect.

4. You may find yourself in a situation where you have a sibling who is entirely different from you, or maybe very like you, in personality. Either way, it

can make it hard to get along. If you find it hard to get along with your sibling, try being tolerant to reduce overall negativity. Resist the urge to try to upset your sibling because it amuses you. Keep in mind that you should always treat others the way you want them to treat you, siblings included.

5. It may also be that you and one or more of your siblings are the best of friends. Most siblings fall somewhere in the middle of being great friends and always arguing with each other. If your sibling is your best friend, you may experience some sadness when things such as one of you getting a boyfriend or girlfriend or leaving for college start to happen. If there are multiple siblings, resist the urge to flaunt your good relationship with the intent of making another sibling feel left out.

6. While all siblings argue, there are some instances where siblings engage in real and severe bullying behaviors. If you have a sibling that is hurting you physically or emotionally, it is just as important to stop it as if it were someone who is not related to you. If your parents dismiss it as sibling rivalry and don't listen to you, you should look for another trusted adult to help you.

7. It may be harder to maintain healthy boundaries with siblings than it is with other people. You may have a sibling that takes your stuff without permission, borrows your clothes and never returns them, or always wants to hang out with you when you are with your friends. Working out some ground rules may be helpful. It is more likely that everyone will follow and acknowledge these rules and boundaries if the entire family is involved in creating them.

8. If you find that one of your siblings tries to be part of your social life and wants to hang with you and

your friends, it might be because they have a harder time than you are making friends on their own. Maybe you could make it a point to include your sibling sometimes, but not all the time. Sometimes the sibling just wants your time and attention; providing that particular time or attention for your sibling can go a long way to keeping them from trying to get your attention by aggravating you.

9. Think about treating your sibling as you would any other friend. What would happen if you did share your stuff, included your sibling in social activities, and hung out just with your sibling to play a favorite game of theirs or give them some advice if they need it?

10. Don't insult your siblings for not being good at something, or put them down because you are better at it than they are. Resisting the urge to do so can be especially hard if you are the oldest and like to feel responsible and in control. It is important to allow your siblings to be themselves, too.

Siblings are the people we practice on, the people who teach us about fairness and cooperation and kindness and caring – quite often the hard way. – Pamela Dugdale

30
Authority Figures

Whether you like it or not, there will always be someone in a position of power over you. Being able to manage interactions with a person of authority will make a significant difference in many aspects of your life.

1. Authority figures appear in many walks of life. At home, it is your parent(s) or another guardian who are the authority figures. At school, it is your teachers, professors, or administrators who are in a position of power over you. At work, your boss or another supervisor in the chain of command plays that role. In the community; police, fire, and other safety personnel have authority over what you can and cannot do.

2. If you look at the examples of authority figures, above, it becomes apparent that experience, knowledge, and training have a great deal to do with the level of authority that someone has. Most authority figures have had to work for or gain experience to have that position.

3. While people in authority may try to command respect from you, it is entirely impossible to force you, or anyone for that matter, to respect someone else. People earn your respect by how they interact with you. However, with people in general, and especially in the case of authority figures, it is best to act and treat them in a polite manner, whether you respect the person or not.

4. It may help to recognize that authority figures *do* hold power, over your curfew, grades, your schedule or promotions at work, and whether you receive a ticket that would hurt your driving record.

5. You may be thinking, "I'll just work for myself and be my own boss." Even in that scenario, there are people in positions of authority. Your customers or clients become your boss.

6. Things will go more smoothly if you use good manners with someone in a position of authority. Nice gets nice in return. Always choose to do the right thing, even when no one is looking. Your actions do speak louder than your words.

7. It is also important to listen carefully to what the person in authority is saying or requesting of you. If you don't understand what they want from you, or if you disagree with them, you should politely ask for clarification or calmly state the problem and share your view.

8. Arguing with any authority figure typically ends badly for the person that isn't in charge. Grounding, detention, or getting a ticket are all examples of how arguing might create a bigger problem than you might have had in the first place. Authority figures can also hold a grudge and make your situation difficult in the long term.

9. Most authority figures, when met with a polite tone of voice, will return the same tone back to you. On the other hand, if you use a rude, snarky, or argumentative tone of voice you will probably receive the same in return.

10. There might be times when a person in authority becomes abusive of the power position they hold. If you feel that is the case, it is best to talk to a trusted adult about what you can or should do. If the problem

is something that should be reported or discussed at a higher level than the person in authority with whom it occurred, be careful to make sure you understand the correct procedure and chain of command for doing so.

The wisest have the most authority. - Plato

31

Peer Pressure

You might experience a lot of pressure to fit in with your peers. It is very common for teenagers to feel that way. In part, it is because you are becoming independent of your parents and maturing into who you want to be as a person. Being strong enough to resist peer pressure can be a challenge because you might want to fit in with the crowd. Remember that a large part of maturity means sticking to your set of rules and beliefs, regardless of what other people are doing.

1. Peer pressure can become intense in the teen years. Here are some of the things that you might experience pressure to do:

    a. help solve someone else's conflict;
    b. smoke, vape, do drugs, drink alcohol, or ingest/consume any other illegal substance;
    c. bully others;
    d. become physically intimate;
    e. do the latest viral dare (eating cinnamon or making yourself pass out);
    f. steal, vandalize, drive without a license, speed, or do any other illegal activity;
    g. haze or harass underclassmen;
    h. post inappropriate content on social media;
    i. cheat on tests or exams;
    j. drive recklessly or too fast to have fun or seem cool; or
    k. have other teens in the car or drive outside of curfew if you are not yet eighteen years old.

2. You might even experience pressure from other teens to do something that is illegal. It might sound exciting to you, but illegal activities could very well land you in court and, if severe enough, even in jail, and you will have a permanent criminal record. Future employers

will see your record as they evaluate you for a job. They will very likely not hire you and move on to someone else with a clean record. Illegal activities can truly have a very long and negative impact on the rest of your life. The thrill of the moment isn't worth the risk.

3. Evaluate the people with who you are spending time. It is better to have no friends for a brief time than to be with friends who are pressuring you to do things that you know aren't in your best interest. These aren't loyal friends.

4. There are groups of teens out there who get together but don't engage in illegal activities. They still have a fun time together but without the added risks. Try to find these groups where you live and look for friends in those groups who share your interests and beliefs. Some schools have a Project Purple Club (http://thpprojectpurple.org/the-project/) where members commit to a list of beliefs. Check the website for more information and learn about The Herren Project. If your school doesn't have one, maybe you could be the person to start one.

5. If you find yourself in a situation that you didn't expect, for example, your friends are smoking or drinking, there is a way to get out gracefully. You can calmly say, "I gotta run, guys. I'll catch you later," or something to that effect. Resist the urge to judge the other teens and try not to react too strongly, even if you feel freaked out inside. Remain relaxed and cool. You can set up a code word to text to your parents if you need to leave somewhere. The code word can let them know you might not be at the house where they dropped you off, but that you will be at another location decided on beforehand. You could also create a code word that you can text them when you want them to call you and say that they need you at home to get yourself out of an uncomfortable situation. It might be important to

inform your parents why you left or wanted to come home if the activity is dangerous or illegal.

6. Never get into a car with someone who has been drinking or using any drugs or substances. Contact your parents or a trusted adult to come pick you up. Create a contract with your parents or another guardian that you won't be in trouble for being out with friends who are drinking or using drugs if you call them to come and get you.

7. Calmly respond to anyone badgering you or using verbal threats to pressure you with the phrase, "It's just not my thing." If you calmly and repeatedly respond with the same phrase and do not show any signs whatsoever that you are caving in to what the person wants you to do, that person pressuring you will most likely give up and stop. If you show a strong reaction or start freaking out and telling everyone what they should or shouldn't do, the other teens might think you are too judgmental and won't want to hang out with you.

8. You might enjoy the attention that you get from the person or group of individuals who are trying to get you to do something that you wouldn't normally do. You could be tempted to do what they want because you want to be friends with them and be part of their crowd. Remember, though, that if a friendship is contingent upon you doing something that isn't true to being yourself, then it isn't a real friendship.

9. If you stay true to your personal values and beliefs, no matter how much you are under pressure, you might find that the people pressuring you will respect you for standing strong against the crowd. Even if they don't, you can still feel good about yourself for doing what feels right for you.

10. Even if a pressure situation upsets you, resist the urge to speak badly of those who pressured you. You might feel like you want to take revenge at the moment, but anything negative things you might say will get back to those people and create bigger problems for you.

May we be different in order to make a difference in the world. - Neal A. Maxwell

32

Attending Funerals and Mourning

As you mature, it becomes increasingly likely that you will have to attend funeral services for someone who has passed away. You might have already had this experience. Funeral services have special rules for how to behave.

1. If the family of the person who has passed has a different religion than your own, it can be helpful to research details regarding the services and particular customs, so you know what to expect.

2. While at services, regardless of religion, observe how others are acting and try to blend in. For example, speak in hushed or whispered tones if others are speaking this way. Your voice and energy levels should match those of everyone else around you. Don't comment in any way about how anyone looks, including the deceased. During a wake, the body of the deceased might be visible in the casket. A dead body usually will appear very pale and wax-like. If it is an open casket wake, and you don't want to see the body, it is okay to choose not to walk by it. If you find that you do have to walk by the casket to greet the family in mourning, it is also okay not to look inside. It is not okay to shield your eyes dramatically. Try not to call attention to yourself in any way.

3. If, on the other hand, you are interested in seeing the body at the wake, don't comment about the person's remains or touch the body. Give careful attention to your facial expression so that it remains somber at that moment. Be sure that you don't give the appearance that you are frightened, disgusted, or joking around.

4. If the line at a wake to greet the family is long, you should wait patiently and don't comment about being bored. When you go through the receiving line where the deceased's loved ones are lined up, shake hands with

all the family members, even if you don't know them personally, and say, "I'm very sorry for your loss." If you do know a family member well, it is appropriate to give them a hug while telling them that you are sorry for their loss.

5. Don't comment on or question how the person died. Don't say any sentence that begins with "at least." If you aren't sure what to say, just repeat that you are sorry for their loss, or say nothing at all. Awkward silences are a part of funerals and are difficult for everyone, but silence is better than filling the gap by saying something that comes out all wrong.

6. Don't laugh loudly or make any loud noises. It is okay to converse very quietly, in small groups.

7. Mourning is a different type of sadness. It is deeper because of the sense of loss you experience. Your grieving experience may be different from others, depending on how close you were to the person who passed away. You may feel more sadness for someone you didn't know very well than you expect, especially if that person was young.

8. Mourning can cause physical sensations. It may feel as though your heart is indeed breaking or that you are carrying something heavy on your back. Some people mourn inwardly, and others grieve outwardly. It is entirely normal to cry if you feel sad, and even scream in private if it makes you feel better. If you are attending a public service, do not scream or wail in a dramatic way while you are there.

9. Mourning can occur around any significant loss, not just the death of someone you love. People can be in mourning over the loss of a pet, a divorce, the loss of a job, or other stressful life events.

10. If you experience a time of mourning for any reason, you might find it comforting to learn more the work of Elisabeth Kubler-Ross. She developed a long-known model of understanding grief and mourning. She shows that grief and mourning have five stages that everyone goes through:

        a. Denial,
        b. Anger,
        c. Bargaining,
        d. Depression, and
        e. Acceptance

A funeral isn't a day in a lifetime; it's a lifetime in a day. - Unknown

Section 3:

Social Media

33

The Almighty Internet

The Internet is truly remarkable. It keeps you connected to friends, allows you to play video games, provides entertainment, and gives you access to endless information.

1. Social media can be an important, and even vital, part of your life. It is one way that you can connect with your friends nearby, and make friends across the globe. Social media is an awesome thing, but it is a powerful and challenging tool that you can use with both positive and negative results. The most important aspect of learning about social media is how to be a good consumer or user, no matter how you use it.

2. When you post something on social media, make it a practice to stop and think for a few seconds before you hit send or post. Ask yourself if it would make your grandmother uncomfortable. If the answer is "yes," or even "maybe," it might be better not to post it. Think about what could happen if you post it anyway, versus what would happen if you don't.

3. Even with "privacy settings," people that you don't know can and do see your postings. Do a search for your name and see what turns up. Make sure that everything you post is suitable for general audiences, including the potential future employer that will be checking your social media accounts.

4. Once something is posted on social media, it leaves a digital footprint that is there forever. Truly forever. Even if you delete it, or it self-destructs after a time, the digital footprint remains. You can never completely erase something that you post on social media.

5. Distasteful posts can affect your ability to get a job. Both of us run companies in addition to writing books together. We always check social media before we hire teenagers. If we see something that turns us off about a person, we move on to another candidate. We guarantee you that other potential employers do the same. They will check your social media accounts.

6. Your parents have probably told you not to post any personal information about yourself online. They say this, not just to be controlling parents, but to protect you from the people online who have criminal intent. We will look more at online safety in the next section, but it is crucial that you not ignore or minimize the fact that putting personal information about yourself online can put you in very real danger.

7. Never post anything on social media when you are feeling highly emotional. If you are lonely, sad, mad, frustrated, irritated, annoyed, or any other negative emotion, wait to post until you are in a more neutral or positive mindset. Regret is another negative emotion that you have the power to avoid making public. The same applies for when you feel elated, in love, or over-the-top happy or excited about something. When you have one of these feelings, you might accidentally share too much. There is an app called ReThink that gives you that extra second to stop and think about whether you should send the text or post the thought before you do it.

8. Remember that online messages don't have a tone of voice and are read by the reader in the tone of voice they imagine in their head. You may have a kidding tone in your mind when you are posting something, but that tone may not be how the other person interprets it when they read the post. An example would be that you may be laughing at someone else's post and comment back, "You are so weird." The person reading

your post might take it literally and believe that you really think that person is weird. You can soften it by adding a smiley emoji, to show that you are joking around. Using emoji's is important to help others understand your meaning.

9. Try not to give too much weight to how many likes or comments you get on a post or status. These things don't in any way determine how much people like you or your self-worth.

10. Creating secret accounts is not the best choice. You may not like adults in your life seeing your social media accounts. We get that, and you certainly don't need to show every post to your parents or other adults. However, having trusted adults able to see your posts can be a good thing. They will see if you have posted something that you shouldn't have or something that could have a negative impact on you that you may not have thought about, and point it out to you. Even if you always try to do your very best to use good judgement about what to post, it doesn't hurt to have an adult who cares about you looking in now and then to make sure.

What happens in Vegas stays in Vegas; what happens on Twitter stays on Google forever. - Jure Klepic

34

Privacy and Personal Information

You may think, once you have privacy settings in place for your social media accounts, that what you post remains available to only you and your friends. The fact is, this is not true. Keep in mind that, even using very strict privacy settings, privacy online is limited, or even non-existent. Consider that anything you post might become public.

1. Keep all your passwords completely private from everyone, except for your parents. Password protection is the most important key to protecting your identity online. Even if a friend shares their password(s) with you, don't ever give them yours, and don't share your friend's password with anyone else. Encourage your friend to change their password(s) and not give it to anyone again, either. Never send a password for anything in an e-mail, text, or on social media. If you do, or if you have in the past, you should change that password immediately. The same goes for your Social Security number, credit card numbers, debit card and PIN numbers, and any types of accounts that have information that people could steal or use against you.

2. Keep your information private as much as you can. Not only will it help stop identity theft, but it will also help protect you from being disrespected, bullied, or from getting negative comments posted about you. You will enjoy your online time more if you know that only those people who have your approval know your confidential information. If anyone pressures you to give up this information, don't give it to them under any circumstances. Any person who forcefully and intensely urges you to share personal information isn't being a loyal friend. Also, you should not put pressure on others to give you their passwords so that you can access gaming sites or other social media.

3. Use passwords that are nearly impossible to guess. Don't use your birthday, consecutive numbers like 1234, the word "password," your pet's name, or anything that is easily identifiable as you or yours. For sensitive information, don't keep passwords on your phone or your computer. Keep your phone locked, and password protected so that only you and your parents can access its contents. If you think that someone has hacked your online accounts, whether they are financial accounts or social media, change your password right away. If you do have a bank account, make sure that you check it frequently to make sure there isn't any activity there that wasn't yours. If there is any suspicious activity, report it to the bank.

4. Everything that you post in a digital form leaves a footprint or fingerprint. If someone wants to know what you have posted, whether you have deleted it or not, that person will be able to find it. Even with apps that make photos or videos disappear, someone can quickly take a screenshot during that brief time that it is visible. Apps may notify you that someone took the screenshot, but not if the person you sent it to takes a picture of their device with another device. There are ways around everything if someone wants to access or share the information and things that you post or send digitally.

5. A normal part of being a teen is wanting your privacy, especially around your friends and away from your parents. A regular part of being a parent wants your child to be safe. One way to keep your private thoughts truly private is to keep a written diary or journal. Family members might want to snoop around and read it, so keep it hidden. Even with that, this way is certainly more private than social media posts.

6. An effective way to check on what is available about you online is to periodically type your name into a search engine, such as Google. It is also possible to set up a search engine alert that sends you an email if your name

shows up online. It is also kind of cool to see who else out there has the same name.

7. This video shows exactly how easy it is to find out personal information about you if someone wants to do so. It isn't just about what you post; it can be what other people post about you, too. http://www.netsmartz.org/RealLifeStories/6DegreesOfInformation.*

8. If you want to have more friends, or a boyfriend or girlfriend, you might be tempted to do things that could compromise your privacy. Sexting, or sending a nude or partially nude photograph of yourself, to a boy or girl friend, may seem like an appropriate thing to do for someone you love, but it is not. Don't do it. Not only is it never a good idea, but it could also have serious legal consequences. Here is another video that can demonstrate how quickly you can lose your privacy this way. http://www.netsmartz.org/RealLifeStories/YourPhotoFate*

9. Typically, the default settings on social media accounts are the most public. Do a check on each social media account you have and make sure that the privacy settings are set to meet your needs. The older you are, the less restricted it needs to be. A 17-year-old who is nearly ready to leave home for school or a job will probably be able to handle social media with fewer restrictions than a 13-year-old.

10. To sum it all up, the very best way to make sure that digital privacy isn't a worry for you is simply never to post or say anything online that you would not want the entire world to see.

*Source: http://www.netsmartz.org

Privacy is one of the biggest problems in this new electronic age. – Andy Grove

35

Friending and Netiquette

Social manners, also called etiquette, are important when using social media. When you are online, social expectations and manners are called netiquette.

1. When you communicate with other people online, always remember that the people reading online content are real people. It can be easy to insult someone from behind a computer or handheld device. People will often post comments online that they would never say face to face. Remember that there is a human being on the other end of any post or remark.

2. If someone communicates with you in a way that is intended to upset you, your best bet is not to respond at all. Online wars can start when you angrily respond to something posted that is meant to upset you. Depending on the nature of the post, it may be harmless and not meant for you to take it personally. For example, if someone posts a comment about their particular political views, this may upset you, but you should not take it personally. On the other hand, if someone is trying to spread a bad rumor about you, this person probably is trying to hurt and upset you. When someone is deliberately setting out to hurt you, it could be cyberbullying. Refer to our section on **Cyberbullying** for more information.

3. Posting nude or partially nude photos of yourself or others online is against the law. These kinds of pictures contain illegal content. You could face criminal charges for sharing or receiving your own or other people's nude or partially nude photos. It is unlawful to even to have them on your phone. Of course, the best way to prevent a problem is not to take these kinds of pictures at all!

4. The number of friends you have on social media is not a measure of how well-liked or popular you are. Don't try to friend people that you don't know just to increase your friend total. It increases your vulnerability to people who might not be who they say they are, and it doesn't increase your popularity in real life in any way.

5. Don't post unflattering photos of others. You wouldn't want unflattering pictures of you posted online, right? So, even if you think it is funny, it won't be worth the laugh when the other person gets upset with you. If you are unsure about posting a photo of someone else, ask them first.

6. If you are near someone's phone or tablet and a notification or message pops up, don't read it. You might even tell the person that you are going to turn the phone face down to respect their privacy.

7. If someone tags you in a post that has content that is rude or offensive, un-tag yourself from that post. You don't need to stay tagged in those kinds of posts.

8. We're sure, like most people, you would love to see a video or post of yours go viral. Let's face it; it is rewarding to see the attention that a post can get. Even so, don't post things that will upset others to achieve viral status.

9. Don't accept friend requests from people you don't know. Being careful about a friend request is especially important if the individual isn't friends with anyone else on your friend's list. Think about why someone who has never met you, or any of your friends, would want to friend you. Many of these types of friend requests are scams and not real people, or not at all the people they say they are. They may even be trying to hack into your account.

10. Don't believe everything you see online. Content might just be someone's opinion, or it might even be flat out incorrect. Just because it is online does not mean that it is true.

Let your Internet engagement show your inner beauty through online actions with Netiquette. – David Chiles

36

Online Presence

Both of us have employed teens and young adults as program assistants at our respective social skills centers. As we mentioned previously, one of the first things we do when we consider hiring a teen is to check out their social media presence and do an Internet search of their name. Checking on social media is now a very widespread practice among employers. And don't forget that your relatives can see your online presence, too!

1. Just like in real life, keep in mind that your online life makes an impression. Maybe even more so, because when you meet someone in person, they see you in a far different context than when they are looking at online pictures and posts.

2. Even if you aren't currently seeking employment or applying to colleges, it is still important that your online life always makes a good impression. It is likely that, at some time in the future, it is going to be a potential employer's, or college admissions officer's, first impression of you.

3. If you are employed or going to school, be careful about posting things that compromise your work or school situation. For example, if you call out sick to work, and then post about the fun time you had at the beach, your employer might see that, and you could lose your job.

4. All sorts of public records are available online, and likely will be there forever. We know a young woman who made some mistakes in the past and got arrested for shoplifting. Even though she has completely changed her life, and now has a college degree, she has had a tough time finding anyone to hire her because the arrest record always pops up in a search of her name.

5. The chances are that you have family members connected to all or some of your social media accounts. Are you sure that picture is one that you want your grandmother to see? You might want to keep the fun stuff that you share with your friends on social media apps that adults don't usually use. However, bear in mind that any fun stuff that you post online should not be content that will hurt you with college or job applications when a potential employer or college admissions officer runs a search of your name.

6. Yes, we agree that your grandma probably should not be on the same social media accounts as your friends. You might want to have two different (but not secret) accounts, one for friends and one for family, or create groups or lists to separate family and friends so that when you post something online, you can choose which group or list can see it.

7. If you have posted things in the past that you may regret in the future, now would be an appropriate time to start cleaning up your social media life. Even though deleted content leaves a footprint, it is less likely that someone would be able to access it if you remove it sooner rather than later.

8. Here is a video about how quickly one post can have an enormous impact on your future.
    http://www.netsmartz.org/RealLifeStories/TwoKindsOfStupid*

9. Even when you feel sure that no adults will see what you have posted, keep in the back of your mind that the people who do see it still might share it with someone that you didn't expect.

10. A friend of ours who is a school counselor explained it to us this way. "It's important to pretend that your profile on social media is the same as a billboard about your life. People are going to drive by that billboard. What would you like them to see?"

It takes 20 years to build a reputation and five minutes to ruin it. If you think about that, you'll do things differently. – Warren Buffett

37

Gaming

Online gaming is a way to connect with friends, make friends across the globe, and even attend a social event without ever leaving your house. And it is super fun! We encourage you to evaluate how much time you spend gaming, and on screen time in general. Make sure that you balance your screen time with some genuine face-to-face time with your family and friends.

1. It is important to think about socializing online in the same way you think about attending any social event or function. If you want other people to hang out with you online, be mindful of how you are acting.

2. Many times, you don't know who you might be playing with or even the ages of those other people. Your online behavior should be tame enough for people of all ages, younger and older.

3. Although you will probably hear a lot of profanity while gaming, excessive use of profanity is unnecessary. You could find yourself banned from a game for swearing. Swearing has a time, place, and use, but it can be a turnoff to other people. Swearing can become a habit, and it is a habit that is hard to break.

4. The same tips apply to using too much trash talk with the other players. A little friendly competition is fun, but too much bragging or putting down the other players might cause you to lose your online friends. If the conversation that is text-based, as many games are, it's important for you to remember that people interpret the text differently. They may misinterpret the way you meant it. Use emoticons or things in parentheses, such as (sarcasm) or (pun intended) so that other players understand your intention more clearly.

5. You may run into new or less experienced players of a game. If you are kind to that person and help them learn the ropes, you might make a new friend. Remember, you were once new to the game, too.

6. Different online games have different rules around quitting a game early. In certain games, it is okay that players leave before the end of the game, but in others, it is considered uncool. Be sure to know the accepted "stay or go" policy for the game you are playing. Ditching other players and not finishing a game, or holding someone back from moving forward because you have been beaten and refuse to quit, might irritate the other players.

7. Changing a rule isn't allowed unless all players agree. However, if a game allows an action, destroying something or stealing from someone else, for example, then that action should be considered a function of the game.

8. Screen cheating, screening, and screen hacking are when someone watches their opponent's moves on a split screen game, whether online or playing in the same room. It is considered uncool.

9. As you would with any guest in your home or hanging out with a friend, think about the other player's comfort level. For example, if you use voice communication when you play a game, make sure there aren't any distracting background noises like loud music or sounds of you eating.

10. Just as with in-person games, unless it is a truly competitive game or sport, social games are just for fun. Be a good sport and end a game you have lost with a gg (good game). It is, however, considered bad manners for a winning player to post a gg for the losing player to make that player leave.

Ever notice that people never say, "It's only a game" when they're winning? – Ivern Ball

38

Sharing Too Much and Annoying Others

The Internet is ideal for sharing, connecting, and communicating with others. You should be cautious, though, about sharing too much.

1. Post about things that other people might care about and not just what is important to you all of the time. Generally speaking, people don't want to see the things that you eat. An exception to this is if you are sharing the recipe. Your friends also don't need to know about **all** the things you do in a day. It might be fun for you to post but not as fun for everyone else to read.

2. In having a conversation online, just like in person, it is best to avoid heated subjects like politics or religion. You may feel passionate about a political or religious view, and believe that you can convince others to agree with your point of view if you post your opinions. It is highly unlikely that any of these types of posts will change anyone's views. It is very likely, however, that your social media contacts will find them annoying.

3. Over sharing personal stuff can make other people uncomfortable. For example, long posts to your girlfriend or boyfriend declaring how much you love that person aren't something you should post online. It is just too personal. Save it for when you are together.

4. It might feel great to get online and vent your feelings, but it is best not to post strong emotions online. If you feel angry or upset, posting your feelings in the heat of the moment might lead to you saying something you regret. Take some time to become calm before posting. A good rule of thumb is to wait 24 hours after an emotional incident before posting online. Talk to a friend in person or using a facetime app rather than posting strong emotions in a public forum.

5. Posting or messaging confusing or vague statements that might need explaining annoy the readers of the post. No one likes guessing games. Also, don't post things that are meant to be humorous but require a certain tone of voice to get the joke. The same goes for private jokes that other people will not understand without the necessary context. Not everyone will read the post using the tone you intended to convey. Emoji's help, but they are not foolproof.

6. Never rant and rave online. It might feel good at the time, but you could get a lot of negative feedback that you must deal with for days or even weeks afterward. Remember that actual people will read what you post, even though you can't see them. Posts that include a lot of complaining are also annoying for others to read. If you can post your "peeve" in a humorous way, then that may not be annoying, but outright complaining is. And if you complain a lot, people get tired of listening to you very quickly. Also, resist the urge to comment on heated posts that other people write. You could be unintentionally hurting people with your comment.

7. Posts that read as though you are looking for compliments are annoying. Stop fishing for them. Refrain from posting things that appear to be boastful or bragging. Share good news sure, but don't go over the top. Also, be happy when your friends share their good stuff but don't try to one-up them with your stuff. Posts that are overly self-deprecating aren't something that anyone wants to read. Everyone makes mistakes. No one wants to read about you beating yourself up about something.

8. Remember that you don't need to comment or post on everything you see others post online. It is fine to scroll by and ignore it.

9. You should only share about yourself and not about others. If your friends and family want something on

social media, they can post it themselves. Don't spread rumors about things that you have heard online, especially because you don't know if it is true.

10. Repeatedly messaging a person when they aren't responding to you can be hugely irritating to that person. There is a reason that they have not responded. If you have texted or messaged someone three times, and they have not responded, don't send anymore texts or messages until you hear back from that person.

I don't know why people are so keen to put the details of their private life in public; they forget that invisibility is a superpower. - Banksy

39

Offline Meeting and Online Predators

The Internet can be a dangerous place because of the real threat of online predators. You need to know how to avoid them or identify them should they contact you.

1. Online predators think with criminal minds, and it is very likely that you don't understand the way they think. They spend all their time trying to figure out ways to harm people, including teens and children. They are very dangerous people, and you should be aware of them and treat them as such. Never post how lonely you are feeling online. It might seem like a way to get some attention from your online friends, but it also shows a vulnerability that is dangerous to share. Online predators look for teens who are feeling lonely and might try to target you.

2. Just because someone online tells you who they are, that does not mean that they are telling you the truth. For example, an online predator will pretend to be your age when you talk to them online, even though they are in actuality, an adult who wants to harm you.

3. If you meet someone new online and they are messaging you with very flattering comments, be suspicious of that person. Even if it feels great to read the compliments, the person may have an intent to harm you.

4. Be very wary and suspicious if someone you have met online starts to talk about your clothing or how you look. If you don't know the person in real life, now is the time to block that person from your account.

5. If anyone asks you to reveal yourself undressing or undressed, <u>never</u> do it and tell a trusted adult right away. You and your parent(s) should report anyone

who asks you to do this by going to
www.cybertipline.org or your local police.

6. Even if someone has not asked you to undress, but
   wants to see your cleavage or upper thigh or any part
   of you that you would typically cover with clothing,
   including your feet, don't do it.

7. Even with your clothes on, don't post in sexually
   suggestive poses. Don't spread your legs, show your
   cleavage, or make kissy faces. If you already have
   these types of images online, delete them.

8. If someone asks you to meet offline, tell a trusted adult
   right away. Do NOT agree to meet the person, no
   matter how much you might want to.

9. If someone you meet online offers to give you gifts or
   makes promises to make your life better, report it to
   your parents or another adult immediately. This person
   only intends to lure you into a situation where they can
   harm you.

10. If someone says they will, or does, show you parts of
    their body that would normally be covered by clothing,
    or makes suggestive or sexual comments or gestures,
    report it to a trusted adult. We know that we are saying
    trusted adult quite a bit, but it is so important that you
    have one or more of them in your life and on your side.
    That person can be a parent, a grandparent, an aunt, a
    school counselor, a teacher, a pastor, or someone else
    in a similar position.

*Online predators befriend adolescents. They become
closer to them than some family members are.   –
Sharon Cooper*

40

Cyberbullying

Cyberbullying is a big concern and is particularly difficult to manage. It is harder to prevent because the bullies have around-the-clock access to their victims, especially if a victim continues to interact with the bully online.

1. Cyberbullying can be any messaging through text, apps, social media, or gaming. It can be in the form of mean comments, spreading rumors, fake profiles, hacking other people's accounts, unauthorized posting of pictures, or any online communication that is intended to belittle or harm someone.

2. Once something has been sent electronically, it is nearly impossible to delete or retrieve. Usually, a victim is aware of this fact, and this knowledge can cause the effects of cyberbullying to be traumatic and long-lasting. Electronic communication can also be retrieved to and used as evidence against a cyberbully.

3. Cyberbullying can also include "creepy" requests for pictures or content that make a victim feel uncomfortable.

4. Cyberbullies feel empowered by hiding behind technology and will do things that they would never feel bold enough to do in person. Cyberbullying can be extremely heinous and cruel.

5. Don't ever respond to cyberbullying. Instead, capture the bullying with printouts and a screenshot with the date and time you received the message so that you can use it as evidence to stop or prosecute the cyberbully. You might believe that a cyberbully can use technology to cover who they are, but keep in mind that

it is always possible to find out where those messages came from by following the digital footprints.

6. Block the phone numbers of any cyberbullies to prevent them from communicating with you. Call your Internet service providers to remove any social media pages that make false or mean comments about you.

7. Contact your school and show the administrators the messages and captures of the bullying so they can address it with the perpetrator. Bullying creates an unsafe environment at school, and your school can intervene through anti-bullying laws, so your school should be made aware of the situation.

8. Cyberbullies may even go so far as to encourage you to harm yourself. DO NOT LISTEN TO THE BULLY. Tell someone right away. Never hurt yourself or anyone else at the direction of a cyberbully. It isn't your fault, they hold no power over you or understanding of you as a person, and the police should become involved.

9. You and your parent(s) should report any illegal activity through http://www.cybertipline.com/.

10. Our tips on this topic include valuable information we found on http://www.netsmartz.org/Cyberbullying. We strongly suggest you and your parents use this resource, especially if you are involved in cyberbullying as either an aggressor or a victim. This site has high quality videos that provide a complete education for teens regarding these important issues.

Let me tell you something. You're worth it. No matter how many times someone has told you otherwise, you really are. - Unknown

Section 4:

The Bigger World of College, Work, and Adulthood

41

Introductions

First impressions are important. When you are introducing yourself to someone new, they will begin to form an opinion about you based on the way you handle the introduction. If meeting new people feels awkward to you, we suggest that you practice this skill to be sure that you start new relationships off on a positive note.

1. When you are introducing yourself to someone, you should look them in the eye, if you can. If you are too uncomfortable making eye contact with someone, try looking at another part of their face that isn't the eyes but is close to them. If you look at their eyebrows or the top of their nose, they may not notice that you were not looking at their eyes.

2. When meeting someone, try to pay attention to the expression you have on your face. Try to look friendly and smile if that feels natural to you, or think positive thoughts so that your face looks pleasant. If you are thinking, "Oh no! I'm not good at meeting people," it will probably show in your facial expression or your body language. Practice in a mirror at home so you can see what a friendly appearance looks and feels like versus what your expression looks like when you aren't feeling friendly.

3. You will be expected to shake the hand of a person you have just met. People tend to read quite a bit into a handshake so doing it well is important. Always put your right hand forward to shake someone's hand. Hold the other person's hand so that your hand fully grasps onto theirs. Don't just shake someone's fingers. It must be the whole hand. Have a firm, but not a hard squeeze, hold on their hand. No one likes a limp or "dead fish" type of handshake. Pump the clasped hand

up and down two times. Any less or more than this could become awkward.

4. While you shake someone's hand with a friendly look on your face, it is likely that you will learn the other person's name at the same time. Either the person you are meeting, or another person who is introducing you will tell you their name. Either way, try to repeat their name out loud, or in your head, or write it down once you are no longer with them, so that you are more likely to remember it later.

5. You will want to tell the person your name during this exchange if there isn't another person to tell the person you are meeting your name. Say your name loud enough to be heard even if you are feeling nervous or uncomfortable meeting someone new.

6. After you make your initial introduction and shake hands, you should follow up with a short conversational phrase. A typical response upon meeting someone and learning the person's name is to say, "It's nice to meet you."

7. After you say, "It's nice to meet you," insert the person's name at the end of your greeting. That might also help you remember their name. If the person is older than you or an authority figure, you should use Mr. or Mrs. followed by their last name. If the individual is a woman, you can choose to use Ms. (pronounced "mizz") followed by their last name.

8. Upon meeting you, the other person will likely use your name as well. If they happen to mispronounce your name, it is best to give them correct pronunciation at that moment. It won't be considered rude or disrespectful, and it will let them know the proper pronunciation of your name.

9. After being introduced, you could use some small talk topics to chat about with the person you have just met. The weather is a typical small talk topic. If you are at an event, you could say, "I've been looking forward to this."

10. When saying goodbye to the person, try to use their name. You can also tell them again that it was nice to meet them and thank them for their time.

A smile is always the best form of introduction. - Unknown

42

Interviews

If you haven't interviewed for a job or college yet, you will be at some point very soon. Doing well in an interview is important, especially if you are interviewing for the job or college of your choice.

1. When you get an interview, make sure that you prepare and have all the paperwork that you need to take with you. This paperwork could include your resume, reference letters, and perhaps even a copy of your driving record if the job involves driving. Know what you need to bring and have it in a folder to bring with you.

2. Do a little online research about the company or college that is interviewing you. Most interviewers will ask if you have any questions. Plan a few questions ahead of time based on your research. "How much will I be paid?" or "Will I be able to take time off?" are NOT questions you should ask an interviewer. It is helpful to role play the interview with someone to practice answering and asking questions that might come up during the actual interview.

3. Make sure that you dress your best. You can get a sense of what the dress code is from a company's website. Even if you know that a company has a very relaxed dress code, for an interview you should wear something that is considered business casual. It is always better to be a little overdressed rather than underdressed. You should be clean, with combed hair and brushed teeth. Bring a breath mint to eat before the interview, but don't use mints or gum during the interview. Apply lip balm before the interview to help keep you from licking your lips.

4. Don't arrive too early and don't arrive late. The best time to arrive is 10 minutes before your scheduled

interview time. If you arrive before then, wait in your car. If for some reason being late is unavoidable, such as being caught in a traffic jam, make sure that you have the phone number of the person who will be interviewing you. Call them to explain what is going on and why you will be late.

5. Don't bring food or coffee with you to the interview. Not only would it be considered rude, but you run the risk of spilling it on yourself before the interview. You can bring bottled water. If the interviewer offers you coffee or water, it is okay to say, "Yes please, that would be nice," but it is just as well to say, "No thank you, I'm all set."

6. Announce yourself quietly to the receptionist or another person who is there to greet you and let them know who you are there to see. Sit quietly in the waiting area and wait to be invited in for your interview. Stay off your phone or, better yet, leave it in the car until the interview is over. If you keep your phone with you, set it to *Do Not Disturb* during the interview.

7. You will probably be nervous. Take some deep breaths to help yourself feel calm. Interviewers are interested in your strengths, but will often ask you what you think your areas of weakness are, or where you have room for improvement. Be ready with the answers to those questions. Some examples of answers to this question could include the fact that you may be too critical and hard on yourself sometimes or that you tend to try to please everyone even though that is impossible. You could also mention you don't have the experience yet with a certain aspect of the job but are looking forward to learning it.

8. When the person who is interviewing you comes out to greet you, it is customary to give a friendly, firm handshake and make eye contact with the interviewer. You can also say, "Nice to meet you."

9. When you are nervous, you might talk too fast, or too much. Try to slow down. Listen fully to the interviewer's question, and then give your answer. If you need a moment to formulate a reply, you can say, "That's a good question, let me think about that for a minute." If you did not understand a question, it is okay to politely say, "I'm sorry, could you repeat the question for me?"

10. At the end of the interview, you are expected to shake hands again and say, "I appreciate your time today. Thank you," or some variation of this.

Job interviews are like first dates. Good impressions count. Awkwardness can occur. Outcomes are unpredictable. - Unknown

43

Babysitting

Most teens find that one of their first paid jobs is babysitting or pet sitting. It is a time when you become responsible for someone else and accountable to another adult who is not your parent.

1. If you are just starting out, you might consider being a mother's helper first. That way, the parent is home while you get used to taking care of the kids. It may even be a way to get started with each new family that you add to your list of babysitting customers. That way, the parent is there in case you have any questions about house rules such as what the kids can and can't have for snacks. The kids are probably not going to tell you the truth about that stuff!

2. You might look to see if a baby sitter certification course you can attend in your local area. You will learn about childcare, first aid, and more. When you tell prospective parents that you have a certification, it will help you get more work.

3. When you do get offered a babysitting job, make sure you write down the date, time, and which family it is for on a calendar or put it in the calendar on your phone so that you don't forget.

4. If the parent asks you how much you charge to babysit, make sure that you know what the going rate is in your area and use that as your hourly rate. If, at the end of the night, a parent wants to pay you more than what you agreed on, take that as a compliment. Accept the extra and say thank you.

5. A question that you might forget to ask is whether the family has any pets, especially dogs. Sometimes a family dog will treat a babysitter as a stranger in the house. It is important to either get to know the dog

beforehand or have the owner crate the dog or otherwise restrict the dog before you come over. If you are pet sitting, it will be helpful if the family writes down the care instructions for the pet or pets so that you can refer to it, as needed.

6. Find out what the kids like to do. You might want to create a babysitting toolkit full of games and other things to bring with you. Kids like to try new things, and they will find your stuff more interesting than their own. If a family doesn't usually have video games, ask if you might bring yours as something special for the kids to do while the parents are away. Just keep in mind that the game should be rated for Everyone, not Mature or any other rating higher than the kids' ages would usually allow.

7. While most parents will tell you to help yourself to any snacks, you may want to consider bringing your own. That way, you are sure to have snacks that you enjoy and won't have to worry about the amounts. If you want to bring a treat for the kids, make sure it is okay with the parents ahead of time.

8. Stay off your phone while you are working. It is best to just put an away message on to let everyone know you are unavailable. Some apps can do just that. You are being paid to give the kids your full and undivided attention. Once they are asleep, being on your phone and texting with your friends is fine.

9. Snooping around someone else's house and through their belongings is not okay. If you need to go through the kitchen cabinets to find a dish for the kids or a snack, that's different. However, stay out of what are considered restricted areas such as bedrooms, offices and bathroom cabinets.

10. If you are driving yourself to the babysitting job, be on time. You might have to remind parents that you have a driving curfew if you are under eighteen years old. If the parents are picking you up, make sure you are ready to go when they get there.

That awkward moment when a two-year-old kid is talking to you, and you can't understand him, so you just sit there and say, "Oh, really?" - Unknown

44

Appointments

When you are a kid, your parent or guardian typically sets up all your appointments and makes sure you get there on time. At some point, it becomes your responsibility to make and keep your appointments.

1. The first few times you call to make an appointment, you might feel a little anxious about what to say. As a first step, listen in or three-way call with your parent or guardian so you can hear what they say.

2. You can then move on to the next step. Have your parent or guardian listen in while *you* make the call yourself. It's completely normal to feel a bit nervous.

3. If someone answers the call, you should say hello and give them your name and the reason for your call.

4. The person scheduling the appointment may offer you a date and time, or they may ask you what a good day or time might be for you to come in. Be prepared with an answer on the best days and times for you.

5. Depending upon the type of appointment you are making, you might be asked to give more information. For example, if you are making a medical appointment, the office person may need your health insurance card information.

6. To help remember the appointment, and to be certain that you have the correct information, repeat the date and time back to the person scheduling the appointment. You should also write it down and add it to the method in which you or your family keeps track of appointments.

7. Thank the person on the other end of the phone for helping you make the appointment before hanging up.

8. If you call for an appointment and are asked to leave a message, it is helpful to leave your name and phone number first. Leaving your contact information first makes it easier for someone to find your number to call you back without listening to the entire message. Also, give the reason for your call. Listen carefully to see if there is any other information you should leave in your message.

9. If you must reschedule or cancel an appointment, it is the best practice to give at least a 24-hour notice. Some practices, such as doctors or dentists, may charge for an appointment cancelled less than 24 hours in advance.

10. If you forget an appointment, you should call to apologize, ask if there is any charge for the missed appointment, and reschedule.

Unfaithfulness in the act of keeping an appointment is an act of clear dishonesty. You may as well borrow a person's money as his time. – Horace Mann

45

Driving

To get to interviews, work, and appointments, you will usually need to drive. There are social skills involved with driving along with the necessary technical skills you need to be behind the wheel of a vehicle. Some of these are for safety, and some of them are good manners when you are on the road.

1. Yours and any passengers' safety should always come first. Make sure that you and all your passengers buckle up. Be firm and refuse to move if all your passengers are not wearing a seat belt. If you have a tough time remembering to buckle up, you should put a visual reminder on the steering wheel or dashboard. You can use a label maker to make one yourself, with whatever note will remind you to buckle up!

2. It is your job as the driver to make sure your passengers are comfortable in the car. Questions such as, "Is the car warm enough?" "Is it too windy with the window down?" "Is the radio the right volume?" and, on a long trip, "Does anyone need a rest stop break?" are important questions for the comfort of your passengers.

3. Don't drive distracted. Being on your phone or another mobile device, eating and drinking, putting on makeup, or any other activity that removes some or all your attention away from handling the vehicle will distract you from driving. For some people, even talking can be a distraction, especially in congested areas or construction zones. If someone is talking to you and you are feeling distracted, politely ask them to wait to speak to you. Staying quiet as necessary also goes for you if you are a passenger. Be careful not to distract your driver.

4. There are things that people do on the road that are annoying and can interfere with other drivers on the road. Make sure that you use your directional signals and drive the speed limit. Going too slow can be just as dangerous as driving too fast. Don't make a turn from the wrong lane, block an intersection, speed out into traffic without stopping and looking, pass in the breakdown lane to get past a long line of traffic, or drive too close and tailgate other drivers. You won't get there any faster.

5. Resist the urge to show off while driving. Speeding up or drag racing is reckless and dangerous. Peeling out and burning rubber may seem cool to do, but it is more annoying to others around you then anything else. It can also get you in trouble with the police.

6. There are times when it is a law that you pull over, and sometimes it is common courtesy. If you encounter a funeral procession, it is courteous to pull over until the entire line of cars has passed. It is the law to pull over to let emergency vehicles and police cars go by, as well as to stop when school buses stop. Always pull over to the right side of the road, never the left.

7. There are other instances where it is important that you not stop and slow down. In the case of a traffic accident, or a breakdown that you see on the side of the road, stopping or slowing down to see what is going on, often referred to as rubbernecking, can be more dangerous and cause further problems.

8. Follow good parking protocol and manners in parking lots. Don't take up two spaces or park a large vehicle in a compact space. Never park in a handicapped space unless you have the legal authority to do so. If you see another car waiting for a space, don't try to steal that space from them. Don't have someone stand in a

space to save it for you. Make sure that you park in between the lines in the middle of the space.

9. There are times when you will become impatient and angry with other drivers on the road. It can be helpful to remind yourself that you don't know what their issue is. Maybe they have a sick animal in the car and are rushing to get to the vet. Try to keep your cool and not engage other drivers in road rage behavior. It isn't worth the potential for injury or getting a ticket. In most states that will increase the cost of your car insurance for a long time.

10. Anytime you are driving a car; there is always the risk of having an accident. You can reduce the risk by following all the safety and social rules of the road, but accidents do happen. If an accident does happen to you, stay calm no matter what is going on. Never leave the scene of an accident. You will need to exchange information with the other driver or have the police assist. You will share your insurance information, name and contact information, and get that same information from others involved. If another driver is upset and yelling at you, don't respond. Call your parents and the police and let them deal with the irate driver. If an accident resulted in an injury, call 911. If no one is injured, and you are still a minor, you should contact your parents right away. The same rules apply if you are pulled over by the police for a traffic violation. It does happen sometimes. Stay calm, keep your hands visible on the wheel, answer the officer respectfully even if he or she gives you a ticket, and let your parents know what happened.

Don't disappoint your driver's ed teacher. – City of Tacoma Safety Campaign

46

Doorways, Hallways, and Elevators

There are hidden rules to not only these areas where people congregate or pass each other but also to maintaining personal space in general.

1. People will give nonverbal feedback if they feel that you are intruding upon their physical or personal space. If other people are leaning away from you, you might be too close. If other people are taking a step back from you, you might be too close.

2. If someone does take a step back, don't take a step forward. If you are unsure if you are too close, take a step back just in case.

3. Imagine something such as a hula hoop around your waist and don't get any closer than that to other people. Use the length of your arm to tell if you are too close. If standing, you should not be any closer than one arm's length from other people.

4. If sitting, measure how close to be with your forearm, the length from your elbow to your fingertips. Don't get any closer than that to other people.

5. If you knock things over, you are too close to those things and need to take a step back. You should also pick up whatever you knocked over.

6. When having a conversation, make sure that you aren't too close to the other person's face. Also, refrain from touching the other person unless you are very close friends and you know that the other person does not mind if you touch them.

7. If you are an individual who needs to move around a lot, be sure to sit or stand where you have enough room to move without bumping into other people.

8. Try not to stand in doorways when having a conversation. It can be very annoying to people who need to pass through an entrance. If you are in a doorway, it is important to be aware if people need to come through the door, to excuse yourself, and to let them pass.

9. When walking in a hallway, or any other form of an aisle, it is important to stay to the right so that other people can pass. Be aware of those around you and next to you, and make sure that you aren't blocking anyone from moving. Do not text and walk. It takes away all your awareness of others, and this can be rude. If someone bumps you in a crowded hallway or another place, think about whether it was on purpose or possibly an accidental bump before you react.

10. Elevators can be a little different with the rules of personal space. Sometimes in a crowded elevator, people are very close to each other. The unwritten rule in elevators is that everyone stands still and faces forward to the door. You should allow anyone who is getting off an elevator to exit before you get in. Letting people off first also applies to buses and subway cars.

Personal space refers to an area with invisible boundaries surrounding a person's body into which intruders may not come. – Robert Sommer

47

Accepting Criticism

Whether it be a teacher or a professor, a boss, a coach, or your parent, you will be exposed to criticism many times in your life. Constructive criticism can be a powerful force that helps you learn and grow.

1. Being criticized can make you feel defensive. After all, someone is telling you what you should do differently, or better. If you can block those defensive thoughts or feelings and listen, you can decide whether the criticism is helpful.

2. There is a difference between constructive criticism and criticism that is meant to be insulting. One is useful to accept; the other is something that you can learn to let go. The way that a person delivers criticism is important. For example, if a coach yells at you to "move your lazy butt down the field," that is insulting. If the coach says, "I'd like to see you work on these drills to increase your speed," that is constructive.

3. People who are good at offering constructive criticism, use a sandwich method. First, they give a compliment on something that a person is doing well, then the criticism, followed by another comment on what is going right. For example, your teacher might say, "I like the idea presented in this paper very much. I'd like to see you put more emphasis on grammar to raise your grade. Overall, this is an impressive job on that topic." Any time you feel that you want to criticize something yourself, use the sandwich method.

4. If you start to feel emotional or defensive, try to pretend that the criticism isn't about you, but someone else. Distancing yourself can help you look at the criticism from a less emotional perspective.

147

5. Think your way through the criticism and decide which parts of it are helpful to you and which parts are the other person's opinion and not something that you want to change in yourself. There are times when you won't agree with someone's criticism of you.

6. Criticism can help you set goals for yourself in areas that you want to improve.

7. Criticism can also teach you what you might need to do to help others understand your perspective.

8. In situations where the criticism is coming from an authority figure, such as professor, boss or coach, it is best not to argue the facts from your perspective, even if you completely disagree. These types of arguments will never end well for you.

9. In the workforce, you will undergo performance reviews. These are meant to help you advance and make you better at your job. Even if your boss has nothing but praise for you, it is always good to ask for constructive criticism and how you might improve.

10. If you decide that you completely disagree, or don't wish to accept the criticism that is coming your way, the best thing to do is to let the person doing the criticizing, especially if it is an authority figure, know that you appreciate their time and input in letting you know their thoughts.

Criticism is information that will help you grow. – Hendrie Weisinger

48

Telephone Etiquette

Even though most of the time you may be communicating through electronic means, there will still be times when you will need to speak on the phone. How you communicate while on the phone is a key factor in how people will think about you and relate to you.

1. Your voicemail message should be friendly and, if you are applying for employment opportunities or to college, sound adult and professional. For example, "Hi, you have reached the voicemail for [your first and last names]. I'm sorry that I can't answer your call now, but please leave a message, and I will call you back as soon as I can. Thank you."

2. When you answer a call, always identify yourself by name. Do not say, "Yeah," or "What's up?"

3. Focus on the conversation that you are having. Try not to have side conversations with other people in the room, answer emails, or otherwise multitask when you are on a work-related or another important call.

4. If you must answer a question or be interrupted while you are on the phone, let the person on the other end of the call know that you are sorry for the interruption, and then thank them for waiting when you return to the call.

5. Background noise can be disruptive to a person on the other end of a call. Try to avoid loud music or other distractions by moving to a quiet spot. You should also not chew gum or eat when talking to someone on the phone.

6. Holding a phone conversation while you are being waited on by a cashier, while a server is taking your

order in a restaurant, waiting in line, or at the counter at places like banks, is only rude. Have your phone conversation when other people aren't trying to interact with you. It is also disturbing to others around you.

7. Pay attention to your tone of voice during the call. If you smile when you are talking to someone, that will come through in your voice.

8. Also, watch the volume of your voice and make sure you aren't speaking too loudly into the phone or too quietly so that the other person has difficulty understanding you.

9. If you need to leave a message for someone, speak clearly. Spelling your name out in your message can be helpful. Provide any information that the voicemail requests that you leave. Leaving your name, followed by your phone number, at the very beginning of the message helps the person find that information quickly in your message before they call you back.

10. Even if you are using a cell phone that leaves a number on the other person's line, always state your phone number as part of the message. The other person may receive several calls and not know which number is yours.

Good manners have much to do with the emotions. To make them ring true, one must feel them, not merely exhibit them. – Amy Vanderbilt

49

Professional Conduct and Work Ethic

How you conduct yourself at work will be an indicator of your future success. Acting in a professional and responsible manner will lead to increases in pay, promotions and, if you ever leave one job for another, will guarantee a good reference. Work ethic refers to how hard someone tries to do an excellent job for an employer. If you successfully apply for and become accepted into the workforce, the expectations that your employer has are adult expectations. When someone is paying you an hourly wage to perform a set of tasks, employers have the right to fire you if you don't do those tasks in a satisfactory way.

1. When entering this adult world, you are expected to arrive on time every day. A few minutes late is still late and never acceptable in the work setting. A few minutes early is better. Be on time for work. Repeat that in your brain. Be on time for work. Nothing upsets a supervisor more than having employees show up late, even just a few minutes late, especially if you are holding a coffee cup or bag from a fast food restaurant in your hand. If you want to stop for food, leave enough time to do so. If something beyond your control happens, such as a traffic jam, call your boss to explain what is going on and why you aren't there yet.

2. You should be freshly showered, and wearing deodorant and clean, unwrinkled clothes to go to work. Follow our tips in the **Personal Hygiene** section in Chapter 1. If you must be at work early, or if you tend to run late, make sure your clothes and other items you need are in order the night before. Time management also means that you must figure out what time to wake up so that you have time to take a shower before you go to work. Your physical self creates a first, fast, and

lasting impression, so you want it to be the best it can be.

3. Watch your language. Some people are offended by swearing. It will not make you sound intelligent or professional, and it has no place in the workplace. Also, don't make sexually suggestive comments while at work. These comments are considered sexual harassment and will cause issues for you, possibly even legal issues.

4. At work, you are expected to stay off your phone unless your phone is needed to do your job or you are on a break. You are also supposed to be and stay, awake while at your job even if it is boring and even if you were up late the night before. You need to perform your job tasks even if you feel tired.

5. Don't tell your employer your problems. They do not want to know that you couldn't sleep well the night before, ran out of gas, or that a family member was in the shower when you wanted to take yours. Leave any grumpiness or negative stuff that is happening to you outside the door when you get to work. Your bad mood has no place at work. If work is what is causing you problems, then it may be time to consider looking for a different job. Employers don't want to hear any excuses from you. They only want you to perform the job that you have been hired to do.

6. As a teenager, your first supervisor could very well be a teenager, too. They may even seem a little power hungry, and may not be pleasant to work for and have as a boss. The expectation is that you do what your employer wants you to do regardless of whether you like your supervisor or not. It might make for a stressful day, but you still need to do the job you were hired to do.

7. Don't complain to your co-workers about aspects of your job that you don't like. This type of negative conversation at work can be very toxic to the work environment and is always discouraged. Others may complain to you, and you can listen, but resist the urge to join in with your stories or add to the negativity. Don't gossip about your co-workers or say mean things behind other people's backs. It is tempting to do so, but one way or another it will get back to that person. If you find yourself caught up in workplace gossip, the best thing to do is to distract the conversation by changing the subject to something else. If that doesn't work, it is best to find a reason to leave the conversation and get back to work.

8. There may be times when the work distribution seems unfair. The expectation is that you are to do the job asked of you even if you don't think it is fair. It might not feel right to you, but you are to do the job. Unfair labor practices regarding the law, however, aren't something that you need to endure. You can find the federal child labor laws can at ttps://www.dol.gov/general/topic/youthlabor. It is also good to be a team player on the job. Offer to help your co-workers when and where you can. Also, don't be afraid to accept help if someone offers it to you. It can be a way to build relationships at work and, quite often, work relationships can turn into friendships. There are going to be times when you disagree with someone at work. Fighting, crying or yelling isn't professional and won't solve the problem. Use our conflict resolution tips, found in the **Conflicts and Disagreements** section, when issues arise at work. If you can't solve it yourself, it is important to follow your workplace's chain of command and go to your supervisor first. If the problem involves your supervisor, make an appointment to talk their supervisor.

9. If you make a mistake at work, own up to it and then work with your supervisor or another co-worker on how to fix it. Lying about things always backfires, so be truthful. While we are talking about honesty, it can be tempting at work to take things that aren't yours, like office supplies, money from a cash register, or a dessert if you work in a restaurant. These types of actions are stealing. People who do this eventually get caught, and will probably be fired or even find themselves in legal trouble. Honesty is always the best policy.

10. If you make the decision to quit a job, there is important etiquette to follow. You must list past employers on new job applications as references and to show a work history. You want them to give you a good reference. The process of quitting a job involves writing a letter of resignation that gives two weeks' notice of your last day of work. Giving notice is important so that your employer has time to try and fill your position with someone else. Your boss might say it is okay to not work for those two weeks but, if it is required, it is important to do so with a good attitude.

Every job is a self-portrait of the person who does it. Autograph your work with excellence. - Unknown

50

Fear of Adulthood

The thought of becoming an adult can be anxiety-provoking. If you experience some anxiety around the transition from having your parents take care of you to taking care of yourself, we want you to know this is normal for people your age.

1. The teen years can feel very stressful. Adult expectations can feel overwhelming as the responsibilities pile up. Take it day by day and just do your best. Ask for help if you need it, and know that you will learn how to manage everything. It may take some time to adjust, but learn from your mistakes and follow advice from others who have been there.

2. You may feel fearful of the thought of being completely responsible for yourself. You may even think that, when you turn 18, your parents are going to tell you that you are on your own. For most parents, this is very far from the truth. Think of your parents as the safety net that is under you while you make this transition.

3. It can be helpful, if you are in your early to mid-teen years, to work at a job and start to pay some of your bills for your mobile devices, clothing, or car insurance, for example. Paying your bills will help you know that you can generate income that will pay for your expenses.

4. Learning to manage your money can also foster a feeling of control. Ask someone to help you learn to balance your bank accounts, fill out a simple tax return, and even try your hand at some savings or investing.

5. You will also be making a lot of decisions during this time of your life regarding college or a career. It is important to remember that while these choices are

important, they are not the final ones. There are always opportunities in life to change your mind and do something else. If you are afraid that you don't know what you are going to do with your life, that is okay. Just make a start and try something.

6. Some teens who are afraid of adulthood can become irritable, especially toward their parents. If this happens, it can be immensely helpful to offload and talk about your fear of growing up with your parents or a trusted adult. No worry is too weird. We promise you; someone else has already had it. You should never worry alone.

7. There is a subconscious sense of loss and sadness that is a natural part of separating from your parents into a fully launched adult. It is entirely normal to feel that sadness, but it is not good to get stuck there. If you are feeling stuck, discuss it with your parents.

8. You may also find yourself in more than the usual amount of conflict with your parents. An increase in arguing is also a normal part of this transition. This added conflict is sometimes necessary to allow both you and your parents to make the break from child to adult.

9. If you have a boyfriend or a girlfriend, you might also feel stress about where that relationship is going, and want to avoid thinking about adult things like marriage and children. The person you are with may or may not end up being the person you marry. We suggest that you focus on creating the best start into adult life that you can for yourself. You will be a terrific life partner for whomever that person ends up being.

10. For some teens, growing up can feel lonely as you realize that eventually, and now sooner than you might have imagined, you will be responsible for yourself and

maybe a family somewhere down the road. Besides your family, many resources are available to help you on the path to independence. There are community courses and college transition courses which you can take. There are career counselors and life coaches who can give you advice.

Everything you want is on the other side of fear. – Jack Canfield

Afterword

The end goal of your teen years is to develop the skills you need to become an independent person. That doesn't mean that you won't always have your family there to support you, but it can be very satisfying to know that you can rely on yourself.

Independence equals freedom. As an adult, you will begin to enjoy the freedoms you didn't have as a teenager. These privileges can include coming and going as you please, eating what you please, staying up as late as you want to and making all your choices for yourself. With this freedom also comes new responsibilities.

Being independent does not, however, mean that you should not be aware of other people who you live with, whether it is still your family or possibly roommates. If you are going to be out late, let someone know so that no one must stay up worrying about you. Being independent and a new adult, while living at home, does not mean that your parents' rules of the house no longer apply to you. If your parents have rules about boyfriends or girlfriends spending the night, cleaning up after yourself, sharing vehicles and putting gas in them if you use them, then it isn't okay for you to defy those rules, even as an adult. It is still your parents' house. If you want to make your own rules, you will need to get your own place.

The more independence you have previously earned by following your parents' rules, the easier moving into full independence will be for you.

If you are still living at home as a young adult, it is vital that you begin to contribute to the expenses of the house immediately upon graduating high school, trade school, or college and getting a job. Your contribution can come in the form of paying your personal expenses, such as your phone and car insurance, as well as contributing a portion of your paycheck towards rent and food. If your parents refuse to take it, you should make it a habit to put that amount of money away in a savings account for when you are ready to get your own place. As an adult, you will quickly have to learn that your money isn't exactly all your money if you want to live on your own.

Finding a job that allows you to live independently may take time. You will likely have to work at a job or two that doesn't pay very well to get started. It is very rare for anyone to leave high school or college and start off with a salary of $100,000 a year, so having that expectation as you launch your career is likely not to be your reality.

Independence includes being able to take care of yourself in many ways. Yes, you can live on take-out food, but it gets expensive. If you don't know how to cook, now would be the time to learn. If cleaning up or doing laundry is something that someone else has always done for you, it is time to learn to do it yourself.

If you have never had to take care of your finances, it is time to learn how to use and balance a bank account, file a simple tax return, and save for retirement. Trust us, if you start saving for retirement from your very first job, you will never have to worry.

As an independent adult, you will be responsible for managing your own time. You will need to take responsibility for getting up on time, getting to work and appointments on time, and leaving enough time for all the tasks that adult life entails.

If you are reading this book while still in your early teens, independence may still seem far away. Your teen years are an important stage to be enjoyed, to learn and practice valuable skills and yes, to sometimes make mistakes. One of the best indicators that you can be a successful, independent adult is to be able to make a mistake, take responsibility, make amends as needed, and learn what to do should a comparable situation arise in the future.

We wish you the best and the brightest of futures!

About the Authors

Donna Shea and Nadine Briggs are both accomplished social educators. They each facilitate friendship groups at their respective centers in Massachusetts. Nadine's center is Simply Social Kids located in Tyngsboro, and Donna's owns The Peter Pan Center for Social and Emotional Growth in Boxborough. Both Nadine and Donna are parents of children with special needs.

Donna and Nadine consult to schools, parent groups, and human service agencies. They are also seasoned public speakers and travel to bring workshops and seminars to schools, conferences, and other venues across the country.

Donna and Nadine are certified in bullying prevention through the Massachusetts Aggression Reduction Center and are creators of the *How to Make & Keep Friends Social Success in School Initiative* to provide classroom training and team building for school systems.

Donna and Nadine would love to hear your feedback on their books, speak with you about providing programming in your area, or keep in touch with you about new books and materials.

Find them on Facebook, Twitter, and LinkedIn

Email them at howtomakeandkeepfriends@gmail.com

Also by Donna and Nadine

We would appreciate it if you would take a minute to review our book on Amazon. We learn a great deal from our readers and their comments!

Made in the USA
Middletown, DE
26 February 2020